Mystic

Cambridge

Charles

Boston

Boston
Harbor

Charles

Neponset

Charles

The Charles River
A History of Greater Boston's Waterway

Ted Clarke

Schiffer Publishing Ltd

4880 Lower Valley Road • Atglen, PA 19310

Schiffer Books are available at special discounts for bulk purchases for sales promotions or premiums. Special editions, including personalized covers, corporate imprints, and excerpts can be created in large quantities for special needs. For more information contact the publisher:

Published by Schiffer Publishing, Ltd.
4880 Lower Valley Road
Atglen, PA 19310
Phone: (610) 593-1777; Fax: (610) 593-2002
E-mail: Info@schifferbooks.com

For the largest selection of fine reference books on this and related subjects, please visit our website at
www.schifferbooks.com
We are always looking for people to write books on new and related subjects. If you have an idea for a book, please
proposals@schifferbooks.com

This book may be purchased from the publisher.
Please try your bookstore first.
You may write for a free catalog.

In Europe, Schiffer books are distributed by
Bushwood Books
6 Marksbury Ave.
Kew Gardens
Surrey TW9 4JF England
Phone: 44 (0) 20 8392 8585; Fax: 44 (0) 20 8392 9876
E-mail: info@bushwoodbooks.co.uk
Website: www.bushwoodbooks.co.uk

Contents

Introduction

There is something in the scenery of a broad river equivalent to culture and civilization.... A river is superior to a lake in its liberating influence. It has motion and indefinite length. A river touching the back of a town is like a wing. It may be unused as yet, but ready to waft it over the world. With its rapid current it is a slightly fluttering wing. River towns are winged towns.

–Henry David Thoreau

In some places, the Charles is one of Thoreau's broad rivers, running through some of his winged towns. But most of the Charles is shallow, and its broadness shows itself only near Boston. It moves slowly through most of its 308 square mile basin, and wends its way only 80 miles through its turning, torturous course. Yet its influence outstrips its power and reach.

In the era of settlement and during the years of development, Greater Boston relied heavily on the usually docile Charles. Its harnessed power spurred the growth of places like Cambridge, Watertown, Waltham, and parts of Newton like Nonantum and the Upper and Lower Falls. It even influenced relatively distant Dedham, where the drop in elevation was quite moderate.

Rivers have determined the locations of cities and population centers throughout history as civilizations sought water sources for all sorts of reasons—navigation, drinking, transportation, power—even beauty. The Nile, the Tigris and Euphrates, the Tiber, and the Thames are a few names associated with major cities.

The Charles does not rank with them, but it has provided Boston and its sister communities with the things furnished by those more storied streams. It also has the attribute of beauty, and it's surprisingly interesting in many places.

The Charles has played a key role in the Boston area, as we shall see. With its brooks and streams and aquifers as well as man-made ponds and lakes, the watershed stretches south and west as far as Norfolk and Bellingham, Franklin and Hopkinton. From that last-named, most distant locus, marathoners race 26 miles every April to downtown Boston, crossing the river's meanderings as they run, and finishing in Back Bay close to where Frederick Law Olmsted and his disciples harnessed the river's flow and began a reclamation project that transformed the mouth of the river and its surrounding areas.

As the Charles finds its mostly pokey way from Hopkinton to Boston, it falls a moderate 350 feet in elevation, most of it gradual as it flows through 23 towns and cities with another dozen or so that contribute tributary brooks to the mainstream. That major current is notably brown, mostly with sediments and tannins added as it brushes along its banks in twists and turns before finding its widest wash as it passes by Harvard Stadium in Allston and prepares for its final sprint to the locks of the dam at its mouth, heralded in its arrival by the grand span of the Bunker Hill-Zakim Bridge before dispersing its glory into the recently reclaimed Boston Harbor.

The river has 400 years' worth of recorded history with some twists and turns of its own. Samuel de Champlain had explored the area in 1605 and found it heavily populated with Native Americans, many using dugout canoes. Champlain probably didn't explore because there were so many native inhabitants and he didn't know whether some would be hostile. The plague of 1615–17 killed about 95% of them.

John Smith, the adventurer who had helped to settle Jamestown, knew a lot about making maps and exploring shorelines, but he was fooled by the width of the river mouth and the tidal flats into thinking this was a mighty continental river that flowed far inland at great width. Needless to say he was wrong.

Like every river in a metropolitan area, the Charles has been plagued by pollution, overrun by floods, and has encroached on civilization. But an amazing part of its story has been the successful upgrade in its ecosystem thanks to the unstinting efforts of organizations and their volunteers.

This narrative will trace the history of the Charles as it was and is, and also the history and development of many of the towns it flows through. The foam of the river will thus contain splashes of local and Boston history. When you at last close the cover, you will have learned a lot. Photographs will show the Charles mostly as it is, but the river and the towns it runs through have a history. They have worked together to bring us to where we are today.

I.

The first area along the Charles to have a European colony was Charlestown where a couple named the Walfords got things started. They came to the shores of North America as part of a settlement in Weymouth, Massachusetts, headed by Sir Robert Gorges, who gave them a charter. Thomas Walford was a blacksmith who settled on West Hill on the Charlestown peninsula between the Charles and Mystic River in 1625.

Like many pioneers, the Walfords wound up with arrows in their backs (metaphorically speaking). Though they did the difficult spadework, like clearing land for settlement and making agreements with the native tribes, they were quickly displaced by Puritans who were "purer" than they. This was a group from Salem who had headed inland on foot, found Charlestown, and accepted the welcoming hands of the Walfords before they banished this early couple to New Hampshire for the dreaded sin of being Episcopalians or Anglicans and not Puritans.

In 1629, Thomas Graves, also from Salem, laid out streets in an elliptical pattern on the slopes of Charlestown's hills, a pattern that remains in the twenty-first century. The first settlers built homes on the peninsula, and within a year the area was flooded with more Puritans as the Great Migration brought 1,500 from England. John Winthrop, the governor, occupied a great house, and a church was established as well. However, the lack of good drinking water caused the bulk of these people to cross the Charles and settle in Boston where William Blaxton was living by himself. Others moved to Watertown and Roxbury.

The Charles River runs west and south through 23 towns and cities

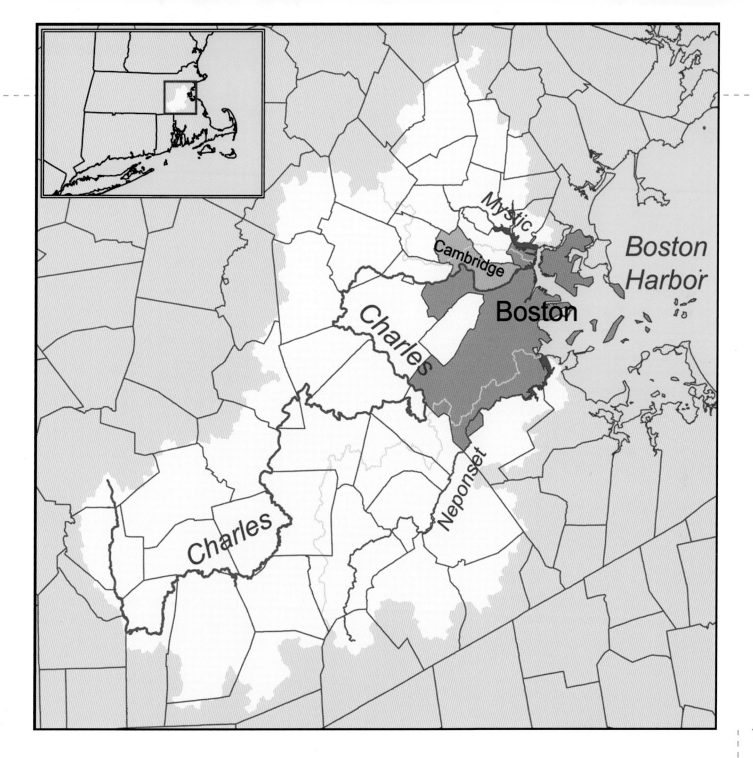

The first settler in the Boston area was a hermit named William Blaxton (or Blackstone) who had come to America with William Gorges in Weymouth. He came to Boston and set up a household on Beacon Hill, near today's Louisburg Square, where there was a fresh water spring.

Blaxton was an ordained minister, but in temperament he was really more like Robinson Crusoe, or perhaps like Henry David Thoreau. He liked his own company and he never got bored. Blaxton had brought about 200 books with him to America, and he brought food, too. One food that worked well on long voyages was apples. They would keep a long time without going bad, and they could just be tossed overboard when you finished them. But not so fast. Blaxton didn't throw them anywhere. He kept the cores and planted an orchard of them where Boston Common is today.

He had been there several years when the Puritans showed up in Charlestown. He'd built a rambling cottage with gables—and a library—and he had fruit to munch on as well as crops he had planted when John Winthrop and his cohorts tried to settle in Charlestown.

They had a hard time getting started because the water wasn't good. From his lofty perch, Blaxton could see their plight and, good Christian that he was, he invited them to come on over—which they did. They readily joined him, but they weren't good neighbors for a loner like Blaxton. The Puritans had their own notion about a city on a hill and it wasn't like Blaxton's. Cities weren't his thing.

They wanted to run things their way, so they just took over for Heaven's sake—or so they believed. Winthrop even brought over the frame of his house from Charlestown—which was a pretty clear sign that he meant to stay. Blaxton was made a freeman, but he put off taking the oath. It gave him no freedom, but made him part of the group, and groups—like cities—weren't his thing.

The Puritans changed the name of the place to Boston, which was all right with Blackstone. They used the Common to graze their cattle and this was OK, too. Then they took most of his land, which wasn't all right. They left him with 50 acres. He said, "No thanks," and sold all but six acres of it back to them, took the money and got out of there.

Blackstone understood that a river offers an opportunity for adventure, and he was due for something different, so he headed west along the Charles. But when he learned that the river curled back on itself, he moved to another stream system, somewhat removed from the Puritans. There he planted another orchard with a new kind of apple called "yellow sweetings." He picked out another hill with a water view. With all his books, he called it "Study Hill." It stood high above a river that would become the Blackstone River in Rhode Island.

Twenty-six years later he returned to Boston, riding his white bull, and married the widow of one of the Puritans with Governor Endicott presiding.

In colonial days, the location of Charlestown gave it a central role in early Massachusetts, especially during the revolution where Paul Revere began his well-chronicled ride to Lexington on April 18, 1775, and where the colonials entrenched themselves at the Battle of Bunker Hill two months later. The British burned Charlestown, but after they were driven out of Boston, people returned and rebuilt with many federal-style homes and buildings, some of which, including Warren Tavern, stand today.

Following the Revolution came a spurt in transportation and industry with the building of thirteen wharves as well as bridges.

At the spot where the British had landed 25 years earlier, the U.S. Navy Yard was built in 1800. The yard became a major employer until President Richard Nixon closed it in 1974. Other uses were found for it, and it is currently a historic attraction, berthing the U.S.S. Constitution.

The first decades of the nineteenth century saw the building of textile mills, especially along the Merrimack River north of Boston, and the Middlesex Canal was built to connect that area with Boston Harbor. Its outlet was on the Mystic River at Charlestown. However, the canal had a short life because the railroad proved a better and cheaper way to

The USS Constitution is docked at Charlestown.

The West Boston Bridge today. It runs from Charles Street to East Cambridge. Also known as the Longfellow Bridge, it is noted for its "salt and pepper shaker" towers.

send freight, and Charlestown, with its wharves on the Mystic and Charles, became the right location for the railroad terminus as well as many new warehouses—it was the place from which everything was shipped everywhere.

All this activity and centralization of transportation had to be connected to the main city of Boston, and as early as 1630 it was—by a ferry. Within a decade, the ferry was run by Harvard College in order to ensure its financial viability. The first bridge was built in 1786 as a toll bridge. It was run by a private group that included John Hancock. The operators had to give Harvard 200 pounds per year to make up for lost income on the ferry.

This bridge across the Charles from what is now the North End of Boston was the longest bridge in America at the time. It was joined by a bridge at the north side of town over the Mystic (1803) leading to the Medford Turnpike through Sullivan Square and Somerville (later Mystic Avenue), and by the Middlesex Canal at the same time. The bridge was a huge success and made more and more money for its stockholders.

Meanwhile, a second bridge was built to span the Charles from West Boston to Cambridge (called the West Boston Bridge). The owners of the original Charles River Bridge complained even though the bridges were 275 yards apart. In compensation, the legislature extended the charter of the first bridge for 30 more years, a period during which it could continue to collect tolls.

But when still another bridge—the Warren Bridge —was given a charter in 1828, very close to the original bridge, the investors sued and the case went as far as the U.S. Supreme Court. The Court took a long time to render a decision, and by that time the Charles River Bridge had closed because its former customers were now using the toll-free Warren Bridge.

The original Charlestown Bridge stood on this spot. This 1899 bridge connects
North Washington Street to Charlestown. The overhead "El" once ran over the
top section of this bridge.

The case was important nationally because it was argued on the basis of eminent domain, and the court under Chief Justice Roger Taney ruled that where the greater good of the public was at stake, it could be given priority over contracts. Taney said that new technology would be unable to flourish if contracts like this were interpreted too broadly. The Supreme Court held that the Charles River Bridge had not specifically been given a monopoly by the original charter, and noted that the "general welfare" would be enhanced by opening a second bridge.

The new bridge brought in still more residents, and the Charles River at this location became less of a barrier than an invitation to expansion.

Charlestown's later history included the building of the Mystic-Tobin Bridge, the elevated train that ran right down Main Street, and later improvements when the elevated was taken down and the stanchions for the Central Artery were placed underground, making room for a new park at City Square.

That area has since become gentrified. Fortunately, a whole section of the town around City Square and Thompson Square had been rebuilt after everything had been burned at the time of Bunker Hill. Many old buildings, and homes remain, especially from the nineteenth century. They still stand along narrow streets and small squares to give the area a unique, pleasant look. The transportation routes, which so dominated Charlestown and diminished it as well, have now been put into "slots" where they are separate from residential areas, and open spaces and parks have been created instead.

Bunker Hill Monument stands on Breed's Hill where the battle was fought. The statue is of Col. William Prescott, the American commander.

Completed in 1876, the Old Charlestown Five Cent Savings Bank at Thompson Square encouraged workers to deposit as little as a nickel to start an account. It now houses offices, but still looks like a bank inside

Warren Tavern (1780) was the first building in the rebuilt Charlestown.

Federal style home on Main Street.

Main Street—a gathering of diverse, but old, buildings

Occasional wide squares vary the cityscape.

Not all Charlestown houses are red brick.

Iron gates and a flight of stairs introduce this brick housing.

Few of these old homes have large lawns, but some have shady gardens.

Details can enhance, such as a window with a sailboat near a shipyard.

The Charles River was not a complete mystery to the early settlers. Many who came to America in the early days used maps drawn by John Smith, the navigator and former colonist of Jamestown, Virginia. Smith explored coastal Massachusetts and Boston Harbor as a landmark in Massachusetts Bay.

Smith's maps had been made as early as 1614, but Smith had called the river "Massachusetts" after the Native American tribe of that name who lived in the area. That name would not stand the test of time nor the royal gaze. Prince Charles, later Charles I of England, changed most of the Indian names that Smith had used, including the river, which he named for himself.

Shortly thereafter, Puritans made their first voyages to America, as part of the "Great Migration" to escape religious and political persecution. They first settled in Salem, but as we have seen, an offshoot of the group walked overland into the interior, finding their way to Charlestown, where settlement along the river began. It had a long history ahead from there.

Charlestown was propitiously situated, but poorly provisioned with fresh water, and when the water proved to be undrinkable, they accepted the invitation of William Blaxton to join him on the Shawmut Peninsula in what would become Boston.

However, both locations were close to the shore and therefore vulnerable to attack by sea or by Native American tribes of the area. These turned out to be needless concerns, but they led to the choice of "New Towne" (later Cambridge) as a capital for the colony.

The Puritan leaders who made that "capital decision" at the end of the year 1630, were part of a huge immigrant group brought by eleven ships including the large *Arabella*. These 700 settlers formed the Massachusetts Bay Colony, and they were cautious because they had left behind a trouble-filled past in the shires of Eastern England. They planned to make their new home a pure religious community without the constraints

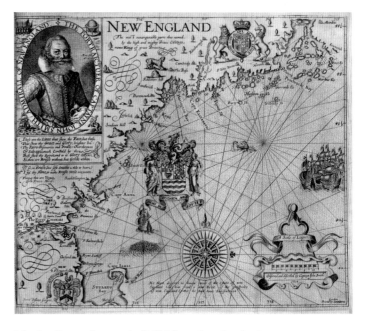

John Smith's maps became the "bible" for early settlers, but he misjudged the Charles.

and bothersome aspects of the Anglican Church, and clearly they planned well, unlike many of the other settlements on the Atlantic Coast of America during this period.

New Towne gained favor in their minds because it was far enough up river that it could not easily be reached by enemy ships. What they couldn't imagine was that the ships that would try to attack it in years to come, would come from their native England.

The governor, John Winthrop, was the main decider and he chose a hill on the north side of the Charles about five miles from its mouth. At that point, a small creek flowed into the river. The river was navigable for ships whose captains knew the likely snares of the narrow channel. Outsiders would lack this advantage and could be reefed and wrecked.

New Towne had another big advantage that Charlestown in particular didn't have—good water. It also was the location of the first good fording place west of Boston, and in a few decades a bridge would be built there to arch the flood of the Charles.

In what would become Cambridge, they set up a plan for a town that would have streets in a grid-like pattern, and in the spring of 1631, they began to put this plan in motion. Moving to a new place and setting up a new capital was a matter of gaining people's confidence. And what usually gets people to act is watching their leaders do the very things that they are asking the followers to do. "Want us to move to New Towne?" they may have thought. "Then you go first."

And they did. Or at least they took steps in that direction. That man with the vision for a "city on a hill," John Winthrop, tried to set an example. He set up a frame of a house—a frame that would go wherever he did, and put it in place where it could be built upon, rather like an "earnest effort." Next, the Deputy-Governor finished his house and moved in with his family. This looked even better, but all was not as it appeared to be.

That fall, the governor had second thoughts. What he did next was almost a retraction. He took down that frame that

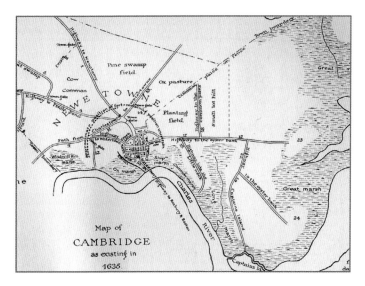

Map of Cambridge, 1636 (Ariel Holmes *The History of Cambridge*)

had looked so symbolic, and he had it set up in Boston instead. "Cambridge-as-capital" began to look doubtful.

Winthrop at this point might remind you a lot of latter-day politicians that you have seen in a different light. He found reasons to back-pedal and flip-flop. He was able to recall an earlier promise that he had made to the people of Boston when they had first settled there that he would remain with the others who were there. Who could deny that a promise was a promise or that old promises trumped new ones?

Those doubters who looked for other issues could find them, certainly. It appears that Winthrop also had received favorable overtures from Chickatawbut, the chief of the Indians of the neighborhood, and was convinced that he was not a threat and that Boston would be just as safe as New Towne, and besides, it was the place that offered the best opportunities for trade.

Winthrop's change of heart posed a dilemma. While many Puritans remained in Newtown, Boston officially became the capital in 1634. So much for New Towne/Cambridge's flirtation with being the seat of government. But that didn't mean that the upriver settlement would come to nothing. Some stayed and made a go of it, and the choice of locale had been based on sound realities by the Puritan-planners. The village where Newtown/Cambridge began is now Harvard Square.

The fledgling village had sensible founders who meant to plant roots and stay. They immediately established a market place where farmers could sell their goods. This was a step beyond what most towns did, but they had the location to make it work. Their town was on the western fringe of what was then civilization, and it was a close commute from there to the harbor and to what would in fact become the capital. In such places, trade centers are often formed.

Though its hub was Harvard, the scope of Newtown was even larger than the Cambridge of today. It included Lexington, known as Cambridge Farms; Arlington, then called West Cambridge (and later Menotomy); and Brighton, known then as Little Cambridge, with Allston lying just south of the same river.

At the time of the founding of Newtown/Cambridge, the trip from there to Boston was eight rather arduous miles: First a ferry took passengers across to what is now North Harvard Street in Allston, then through Brookline and Roxbury to Boston Neck where today's Washington Street is located in the South End. This long trip would be shortened soon. The Great Bridge, built in 1662, made the trip somewhat shorter, but not by much. It eliminated the ferry ride.

Some consider the story of Cambridge to be the story of Harvard, and the two are certainly intertwined. But there's more to Cambridge than just its world-renowned university, established there in 1636—not long after the town itself had been "planted"—as those agrarian types liked to say. Graduates will tell you that the school is America's finest, but even "Yalies" can't deny that it was America's first.

The establishment of the university also cleared up that ambiguity about "Newtown/Cambridge." In 1638, the town was named "Cambridge" at the behest of the many Harvard notables who were graduates of the great English university. These included Governor Winthrop; John Harvard, its major benefactor; Harry Dunster, first president of the college; and Nathaniel Eaton, its first schoolmaster.

Despite its coming prominence as a college town, Cambridge remained mostly a farming village with homes and shops gathered around the common and the college. Most of those who lived in the village were descendants of the original settlers, and as conflicts began between locals and crown officials, the community was mainly in the Patriot camp of farmers, artisans, and tradesmen.

But there were significant exceptions. A few wealthy loyalists had found the town to be a likely spot for erecting magnificent homes—large ones, built along Tory Row (today's Brattle Street), near the place where the river today takes a lengthy loop. These Tories attended the Anglican Church, and took little interest in village affairs, and their incomes did not come from laboring in the community. They also lived in the best neighborhood in town, close to the river to be sure, but also not far from the main thoroughfare, which is today's Massachusetts Avenue.

Those who lived even closer were awakened with alarm on the night of April 18, 1775, by the stirring hoof beats and strident calls of William Dawes as he and his steed made their way to Lexington with a warning of General Gage's foray of redcoats

Brattle Street was known as Tory Row and still has fine mansions.

headed there to capture Sam Adams and John Hancock before heading on to Concord to steal the military stores of the patriots who were stashing them there.

Dawes had crossed the Great Bridge into Cambridge after traveling across the Neck and through Roxbury, Brookline, and Allston. (When the British returned from Lexington, they found that patriots in Cambridge had torn the planks from Great Bridge, so they returned to Boston via Charlestown instead.)

On that afternoon of April 19th, Cambridge patriots fought a skirmish against British regulars at Massachusetts and Rindge Avenues, not far from Davis Square, today's posh part of neighboring Somerville. Four Cambridge men expired in that action, and when the British scurried back to Boston with their once-proud tails now tattered and between their legs, the Patriots of Cambridge and Middlesex County did not relent. Now infuriated by the king and his red-liveried lackeys, they laid siege to embattled Boston and penned up the British in the place that Winthrop had made the capital.

Just a bit farther up the Charles, the Massachusetts Provisional Government met in Watertown while the colonial army had its headquarters at Harvard, whose noble dorms now made convenient barracks for militiamen. Besides that colonial-style reuse of college buildings, those estates that were once the glory of the Tory were now confiscated per order of the Provisional Congress. Chief among them was the Craigie-Vassal House (later the estate of Henry Wadsworth Longfellow), used by George Washington for four months after he arrived on July 3rd to take command of the army.

Upon his arrival, the new commander could see that an attack on Boston could not easily be made without cannons, but he set about inspecting fortifications as defense against any British attack.

Washington, from his early days in the French and Indian conflicts, had always been big on fortifications, and decided to put his men to work improving those that existed. At the same time he added three earthen work forts along the Charles on the Cambridge side, near Putnam Ave., and one at Cottage Farm on the Brookline side. Fort Washington still exists in the Cambridgeport section of the city.

Prior to taking Dorchester Heights and forcing the British to leave Boston, the besieging Americans created a diversion with artillery bursts from Lechmere Point in East Cambridge, destroying some houses in Boston in the process. The troops then left Cambridge for the fortifications on the hills of South Boston until His Majesty's forces had evacuated.

Following the Revolution, the population of the town began to shift somewhat when the West Boston Bridge was built in 1793, giving direct access from Cambridge to Boston (near Charles Street). That eight-mile distance through the Neck was now displaced by a more direct route of only three miles. (In this case the river had been a barrier to progress rather than an adjunct to transportation.)

The word "bridge" has a meaning apart from naming a physical structure. As a verb it suggests the bringing together of people or things that had been separate. The bridges that spanned the Charles had this effect on parts of Cambridge. They led to

Ft. Washington, Cambridgeport

development of additional areas and a strengthening of the town as a whole.

For example, the section called Cambridgeport, between the present Central Square and the river, developed along the roads that led from the new bridge, and Central Square itself grew to become Cambridge's new downtown. It was surrounded at that time by residential streets. A second bridge, the Canal Bridge, was built in 1809 next to the Middlesex Canal, which had just been completed from the northern part of the state. This bridge, too, energized the eastern part of Cambridge and further tied the town together. A glance at a map will show that the leading thoroughfares cut diagonally through the various sections.

Further changes were made, some more gradual and less dramatic than the sprouting up of villages. The bridges and the new roads that led from them into the interior, changed marshland and estates into residential and then industrial areas.

East Cambridge has long been a commercial/industrial area. Building reuse is common.

Turnpikes were added, too, leading to all parts of Cambridge and to adjacent towns. Most of them still exist as major roadways. Those were followed by railroads with the accompanying development of Porter Square and of Somerville and outlying areas of Charlestown.

In 1846 Cambridge became a city and in the last half of the nineteenth century it took on many of the characteristics it would carry into the twentieth century and beyond. These included development of residential areas along the turnpikes and working-class neighborhoods around the industrial sections, especially in East Cambridge and near the brickworks in North Cambridge at Alewife Brook. Beacon Hill's Frederic Tudor began an ice-cutting industry at Fresh Pond, and there was also new housing for immigrants, of whom the Irish were the chief component.

The arrival of the Irish followed the potato blight of the late 1840s, when thousands came to the area and lived in crowded cottages near factories. Within a few years they made up nearly a fourth of the population. Other immigrants came from Italy, Poland, and Portugal around 1900, as well as French Canadians and Russian Jews.

The New England Glass Company, founded in Cambridge in 1818, became the largest glass manufacturer in the world, but seventy years later it moved to Toledo, Ohio. Another company that led the world in the manufacture of its product was Carter Ink, located near the mouth of the Charles. Cambridge became one of the nation's leading industrial cities in the twentieth century, with a population that reached 120,000 before going the other way in the middle of the century when it lost many of its industries.

Harvard and then M.I.T. (the Massachusetts Institute of Technology) began to dominate the city and its culture, particularly as an intellectual center. This change was joined, toward the end of the twentieth and into the twenty-first century, by technology and then biotech firms and other startups, at the same time becoming smaller in population and a more expensive place to live.

Cambridgeport runs from the Charles north to Central Square.

Massachusetts Institute of Technology owns vast areas in Cambridge.

Much of this activity takes place along the Charles, the erstwhile capital of Mass Bay Colony and now the capital of intellectual thought and innovation. These two great universities do not, however, forget the river that passes at their feet. Both use the river for nautical pursuits as well, plying it regularly in their boating activities, which they share with other institutions and the public in general.

Harvard University has spread on both sides of the river.

Brookline owned a shore of the Charles River until that area was ceded to Boston in 1874 so that Brighton, which had become part of Boston, could be connected with the Back Bay. The Brookline border is now on the other side of Commonwealth Avenue.

Originally called "Muddy River," the town of Brookline was used by Boston as a cow pasture before Back Bay was filled. By 1660, the village had about 25 families and in 1705, Brookline became a town. It was a farming community that sold its products in Boston, but by 1800 farmers sold their land to wealthy men who wanted country estates. The railroad and then the streetcar made it a residential suburb.

During the American Revolution, a battle took place in the Cottage Farm part of what was then the Brookline shore of the Charles. It is a little known skirmish, but the outcome was significant because it precluded a British invasion of the hinterlands by using the Charles River Basin, as Governor Winthrop had feared foreign vessels might do years before.

Recall that when he arrived in Cambridge shortly after the Battles of Concord and Lexington, General Washington had shown concern about the possibility of a British naval squadron sailing up the Charles and outflanking the American positions in Cambridge.

The Americans had built redoubts, earthenwork forts and batteries throughout Roxbury, Cambridge, Somerville, and Medford as they began a siege of Boston that would last almost a year.

However, this defense had an obvious weak point and that was the Charles. If the British could get their warships in place along the river they could provide covering fire and transport for soldiers to thrust into the interior, hitting Cambridge where the army headquarters was located at Harvard and Tory Row, and also could strike Watertown, which was the seat of the provincial government.

Small forts in Cambridge were built, one at Cambridgeport, known as Fort Washington, on a height just above the river. Its still exists as a city park. There were also small forts at the tidal marsh north of there and two small ones near today's intersection of River Street and Putnam Avenue.

But the largest and best American fort was on the south side of the Charles. It was called Fort Brookline and it stood at Cottage Farm, about where the Boston University Bridge spans the river today. The point of land there had a view commanding the river and was easily defensible from a land force because it had water or marshland on three sides.

It was here that the wide Charles River Basin and Back Bay narrowed. Any warship heading up the Charles would be slowed at that point and would come under the guns of Fort Brookline, so the British had to reduce it if they were to make such a raid. When the Americans fortified Charlestown and were driven off in the Battle of Bunker Hill, such an assault was a logical next step. At that time the fort had been partially finished by workers under Col. Rufus Putnam, including a wall facing Boston and breastworks along each side. About 500 men had been assigned to complete the building and provide defense.

On July 31, 1775, the British assaulted both Roxbury and Lechmere's Point in East Cambridge without real gain, and then began an attack on the unfinished Fort Brookline, bombarding it heavily first. The Americans did not return fire, but just dug in. The British then sent two floating batteries against the fort, each carrying a 24-pound cannon. They came to within 300 yards but it was getting dark, and they decided to fire from that distance before darkness precluded success. The American commander did not believe he had guns that could reach the British, but the fort put out all the lights and withstood the firing as the British cannonballs missed their mark and the enemy force, exasperated and unsuccessful, withdrew. Washington disagreed with the notion that the American guns could not have damaged the British. He had the commander arrested and he was tried and dismissed from the service.

Nonetheless, the defense at Fort Brookline put an end to British attempts to send a naval force up the Charles. Governor Winthrop and his cohorts had thought the river would be difficult for warships to navigate. He hadn't thought those ships might be English, but he was right about the difficulty.

Ft. Washington, in Cambridgeport, dates from the Revolution. The cannons are 18-pounders

The resource building for this national historic site across Waverly Sreet.

Cottage Farm, where the river makes a bend, was the site of Ft. Brookline.

Boston University/Cottage Farm Bridge crosses from Brookline/Allston into Cambridgeport. Railroad yards at top.

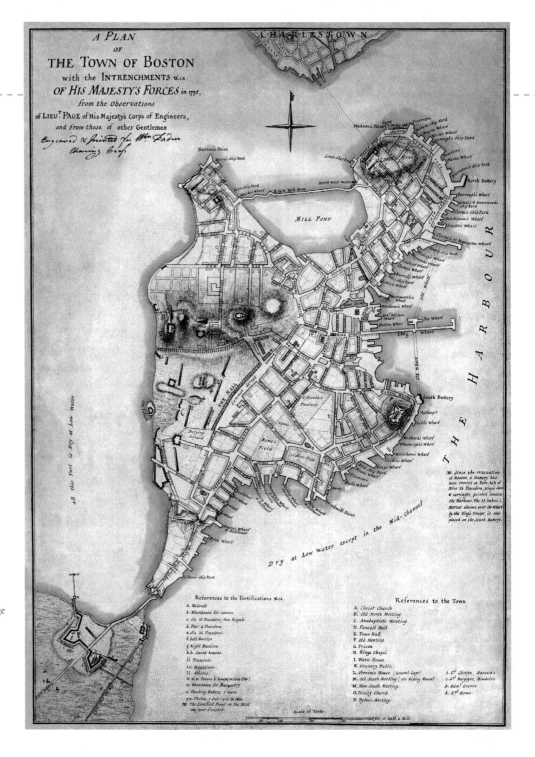

In 1775, Boston was a peninsula with the huge Back Bay on its west.

Most people know that Boston's Back Bay was built on filled-in land. It was not only a bay, but it was large and wide. Before it was filled in, Back Bay was often called "Great Bay." If you were John Smith or Samuel de Champlain and your ship was standing in Boston Harbor as you peered upriver through your glass, you might well have considered the Charles a great river, as they did.

To get some idea of Back Bay's expanse, consider that it stretched east to west from the corner of today's Beacon Street and Charles (where the fictional Mrs. Mallard and her ducklings crossed and where the Public Garden begins) to approximately Kenmore Square. North to south, the water reached from Cambridge to about where the Museum of Fine Arts is located on Huntington Avenue.

Replacing all this water with usable land was a massive, ambitious, and daunting engineering feat, the most amazing of its time. It was needed. Boston's population was growing fast and would grow larger and faster as immigration took hold. Residential land was needed. The Charles River Basin was also a smelly, disease-ridden area, especially at low tide.

However, the reason given for undertaking the project turned out to be none of these, and in the end it was a non-starter. Mill dams were to be built in order to provide power for industry, but that industry never took hold. It went instead elsewhere on the Charles. Little of it came to Back Bay; most of it went to Waltham.

A first mill dam was to be built along the course of Beacon Street, nearly a mile and a half to Sewall's Point, near today's Kenmore Square. It would have a toll road atop it.

A cross dam would also be built to a point near Hemenway Street, creating two basins—a westerly full basin and an easterly receiving basin. At high tide, water would flow through the Full Basin gates and also through sluiceways with turbines in the Cross Dam. That would power the mills that were to be built along the "Roxbury" shore. The water that passed through the cross dam would enter the Receiving Basin and at low tide would flow out again through a second set of gates in the Mill Dam.

The Boston and Roxbury Mill Dam project was completed by 1821. It did provide a more direct route to towns such as Brighton, Brookline, Newton, and Watertown. It saved many miles when traveling from Boston, across the neck and Roxbury, Brookline, and Allston, to the Charles where it could be crossed.

After 1835, railroads would also cross these basins on embankments and trains ran from Worcester and Providence to Back Bay Station. They slowed the flow of water, so there wasn't sufficient power to drive mills. All this criss-crossing also created stagnant pools, so more work was needed.

Back Bay was crossed by railroads and a mill dam.

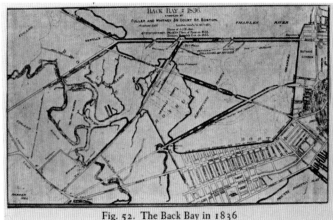

Fig. 52. The Back Bay in 1836

It was agreed, in 1854, to fill in the land south of the river using gravel that would be transported by trains of the Charles River Railroad from East Needham. Trains of 35 cars each could be loaded in ten minutes using new steam shovels. Three trains used a single track and they went around the clock every day of the week, 25 trips per day, filling in 53 acres from 1858–1864.

The area to the west—the Fenway and Longwood areas—had already been filled in when the Back Bay filling began, followed by the setting off of house lots and building of houses that took place in Back Bay to create homes for the wealthy, a project that took about 30 years. All these projects added 570 acres of valuable land from what had been the Charles and its inlets.

The filling of the area between the Public Gardens and Charlesgate began in 1857 and its filling began in the east. So did the establishment of house lots and the building of houses.

Filling followed a routine. First they would lay down the Needham gravel—three and a half feet of it, with soil spread on top. The gravel provided drainage and also stability. It had traveled nine miles over those causeways built for the mills, though on a track that ran parallel to those used by regular trains. William Ort deserves credit for the relative speed of the gravel transit. It was he who invented the steam shovel in 1835.

There were also swivel-style hopper cars on the trains that allowed workers to fill them in just two scoops. These cars were brought right up to the place the gravel was being extracted from cliffs. The operators would then scoop and elevate, and turn toward the train cars. In this precision operation, the bottom of the shovel would open, the gravel would drain into the train car and the whole operation would be over and done in a scant ten minutes—efficiency worthy of a twentieth-century assembly line.

Had it all been done by hand as so much labor was at that time, it would have required 200 workers just to level these hills of gravel that were 50 feet or more in height. The mechanized operation leveled them to about twelve acres of flatland.

The filled trains rolled nine miles to the Back Bay where their contents were downloaded onto smaller, horse-drawn cars which were pulled over spur tracks on top of embankments that were constantly extended (by hand) in several directions until the filling was done. It was a side-by-side illustration of a primitive, labor-intensive operation following one that was state-of-the-art for its day.

Back Bay Fens, an Olmsted project, runs from the Museum of Fine Arts on the left to near Fenway Park at right.

To measure the speed of the development, we can say that all these train deliveries and filling of house lots brought into existence about two house lots every day as a nineteenth-century neighborhood (mostly Victorian in its architecture) arose west of Boston proper. By 1882, Back Bay had been filled and by 1890 the filling had reached Kenmore Square. By the end of that decade, special work in the Back Bay Fens had also been done. Boston was twice as big as it had been when all this started. This was the largest landfill operation ever undertaken in the United States.

In 1910, a dam was built near the mouth of the Charles and that turned the Fens into a freshwater area. With the completion of the Back Bay Fens, the area no longer flooded, but took the overflow from Muddy River and Stony Brook as well as overflows from sewers and storm drains and deposited it safely in the Charles. The 1910 dam near the present Museum of Science was in turn replaced by a newer dam downstream close to the mouth of the river.

Back Bay homes were built as land was filled in during the second half of the nineteenth century.

7.

Across the river from Cambridge and Watertown, the community of Allston-Brighton existed as part of Cambridge for 160 years, its few families toiling mainly in agriculture. At about the same time, just west of Brighton, on Nonantum Hill in Newton, Rev. John Eliot first established a village of "Praying Indians" in 1646.

The earliest families crossed over from Cambridge and their settlement was called "Little Cambridge" which became a prosperous farming community during the 1700s with fewer than 300 people, some of them wealthy Bostonians.

With the outbreak of the Revolution, Little Cambridge established a cattle market to furnish beef to the Continental Army, quartered in and around Harvard and the north side of the Charles. This was a turning point in Brighton history since the cattle trade would become a mainstay for the town. The key traders were John Winship and his son. Their entrepreneurship paid off, and after the war, business not only continued but Brighton became the major trading post in all of Massachusetts for meatpacking.

Brighton continued in that role after the war, even after separating from Cambridge and becoming an independent town in 1807. By that time, the cattle and slaughtering business was dominant, and it was Cambridge's failure to make improvements that were important to the transportation of this industry, that led to Brighton's leaving this union. Cambridge failed to replace the bridge between the Harvard area and Little Cambridge, and this caused real problems.

The availability of a bridge to take people in and out of Cambridge seemed a minor thing to Cantabridgians. But to those in the cattle trade in Brighton, it was a big deal because it threatened the thriving industry they depended on.

They decided to secede and in 1807, got the approval of the legislature and called themselves "Brighton."

That turned out to be a good move because in the next two decades Brighton became a top business center. The Massachusetts Society for Promoting Agriculture built a hall and fair grounds on a hill above Brighton Center, and every fall a cattle show and agricultural fair was held there—the largest event of its type in the state. Brighton achieved this prominence because it was well positioned between Boston and the western towns. It was on the Charles River and on the main line of the Boston and Worcester Railroad while it also had roads that led to Cambridge, Brookline, Roxbury, and Watertown.

A good location is one thing, using it wisely is another. Fortunately for Brighton, at this point it had town leaders who exploited that location—as good entrepreneurs have always done. They brought in industries that fit the location and used its natural assets. For example, Allston, the eastern section of town, had good soil for farming and was near Boston where the things it grew could be sold. When a milldam with a road atop it was built over the Back Bay, access was even easier.

At the same time, the cattle trade grew up around the 100-room Cattle Fair Hotel in Brighton Center and spread out from there. The manager, Zachariah Porter, was a smooth operator. Porter later founded the Porter House Hotel in Cambridge whose name is today also associated with the square and with the Porterhouse steak. But the Cattle Fair was only one of fifteen hotels in and around Brighton Center. Many were famous for their well-stocked bars and, less attractively, for their patrons' rowdy behavior.

All this, despite its profitability, did not suit a town that desired to be residential. The rowdyism depressed real estate prices and so did the stockyards, especially their odors.

On market days, the aptly named Market Street, as well as Washington Street, swarmed with drovers and dealers and herds. The hotels were filled with dealers, and behind the hotels, the stockyards were filled with bovines to buy and sell. By the time of the Civil War, the town had 40 slaughterhouses and factories that made things like tallow and fertilizer. But all this messy activity in the town center was a negative, so the industry agreed to build a single stockyard with a huge slaughterhouse down by the river in North Brighton where the railroad had a stop. Standards of cleanliness and safety could be raised, animals treated more humanely, and that would leave Brighton Center for houses and stores instead of heavy industry.

From Brighton Center west to Oak Square and Nonantum Hill, market gardening took hold with vegetables and fruits grown on small farms sold at roadside stands or nearby markets. Some of the produce was grown in greenhouses, which also grew flowers, even during the winter months when the windows trapped solar radiation and allowed the plants to absorb it. So in the middle of the 1800s, Brighton became a horticultural center as well. Some of the companies that began at that time still operate today. It even had vineyards.

Brighton appeared to be in an upward movement. But leaders tried to do too much too quickly, and some wanted to make personal profits by selling real estate at high prices. They used the momentum brought about by moving the stockyards to improve things like roads, utilities, parks, and sewerage, as well as providing the best firefighting equipment and good schools, and they wanted to erect proud public buildings, too—quickly.

To finance all this they borrowed money—four dollars for every dollar of revenue—and at high lending rates. This deficit spending left Brighton's debt eight times worse than it had ever been, and considerable red ink in just four years. This idea has been tried many times with many failures, and this was no different.

The piper must be paid, and the price would be the loss of their independence. They decided to let someone else pay for their profligate spending. In the period following the Civil War, Boston was grabbing up most of the towns around it, and Brighton was on their list. When it was annexed, Boston would own the debt, which must have given them a comforting feeling, so the citizenry voted four to one to become part of the big city, and on January 1, 1874, it did.

Brighton was also tied closer to Boston by various means of transportation. First there was the extension of trolley lines along Commonwealth Avenue and Brighton Avenue. The areas near those lines became residential as well as commercial. Commonwealth Avenue in particular built many substantial apartment buildings, some of them quite grand.

The railroad also played a major role in development. It had two stops in Brighton and one in Allston, with H.H. Richardson-designed stations, as well as a rail yard in Allston, which had another tie with Cambridge as well. Allston was named for Cambridge landscape painter Washington Allston, the only town in the country named for a painter.

The railroad had made a lot of money from the cattle trade and had improved its operation with the rail yards, a classification yard, repair shops, and two roundhouses.

The trolley line to Brighton divided from the one that ran to Allston at a place called Packard's Conner. Commonweatlh Avenue veered left there and Brighton Avenue went straight ahead to Union Square and from there North Beacon Street ran to Watertown. The stretch from Watertown back to Kenmore Square became a haven for automobile dealers, car parts, and automobile repair shops of all types.

The Allston-Brighton section is home now to many college students as well as immigrant groups. The stockyards are long gone, and the automobile dealers are no longer dominant, all but a few dealers having moved to the suburbs. Even the fabulous Packard Building is now condominiums. Through it all, the Charles flows on, and the Allston-Brighton shoreline of the Charles is one of the longest. The river is quite wide here, and it has all kinds of recreational opportunities. Watercraft and wildlife of many kinds are always about.

Along the Charles
in Brighton: a yacht
passes Northeastern
University Boathouse.

The Skating Club of Boston, long a river
landmark, plans to move shortly.

Mass Turnpike runs parallel to the river past the railroad yards to Brighton and beyond.

Geese cluster near shore in Brighton.

Rowers practice along the Brighton shore.

Boats at Brighton

Brighton

Artesani
Playground, Brighton

Herter Park

8

Elizabeth Shaw Craigie's name doesn't jump off the pages of American history texts or even accounts of Cambridge history. Elizabeth wasn't even someone who had the respect of those who lived near her along the Charles River in her Cambridge neighborhood, known derisively as "Tory Row" because so many loyalists or British sympathizers had lived there before the Revolution.

Elizabeth, a widow who was badly in debt, used to sit in the window that faced the river reading the works of Voltaire. Despite this seemingly odd proclivity and her lack of prominence in the Cantabridgian culture of the moment, Mrs. Craigie could reflect back on some interesting times in her life, and the house she owned had many of these times both behind and ahead of it.

People in Cambridge in the early nineteenth century who sat at home reading the writings of the French philosopher Voltaire were seen as odd to say the least in the early days of the Republic, and the widow of Andrew Craigie, owner of the mansion on "Tory Row" on Brattle Street, not only read from the Frenchman's voluminous tomes, but also rented rooms in the swaggering home that had once housed George Washington. Those things were enough to create a sand-in-the-oyster-shell disturbance that would give Mrs. Craigie a mother-of-pearl patina and bring her name to these pages.

The home deserves that kind of attention at least as well. Its confines would ensure the growth of literary traditions by letting rooms to Henry Wadsworth Longfellow, then a fledgling Harvard professor, who would later own the home. Today the Craigie-Longfellow House is a National Historic Site.

Tory Row stands yet on the western end of Cambridge, near Mt. Auburn Cemetery, the Charles River, and the border with Watertown. Like most of Cambridge, it lies just across the river from Boston, in this case Allston-Brighton. Cambridge was, in those days, home to Harvard and much else. One of its leading figures was a poet; in fact Henry Wadsworth Longfellow became the most popular poet of his day, a popularity that continued into the first part of the twentieth century. He would become owner of the Craigie House. Longellow's story is fascinating; that of the house perhaps more so.

Let's start with the house because its story is older. The house goes back to 1759 when it was built by Col. John Vassall, Jr. whose family used it as a summer residence until just before the Revolution. Vassall was a merchant who became wealthy in the West Indies trade, and he wanted a house with a clear view of the Charles. Only a green lawn separated the two. At that time Vassall felt unsafe in the house and its neighborhood. That was because he was a Loyalist. That is, he remained loyal to the king and parliament, opposed to groups like the Sons of Liberty, and like many in this wealthy neighborhood called "Tory Row," felt compelled to flee to the safety of Boston where British troops could protect them.

The Vassalls kept slaves (Tony and Cuba) in the house and they remained, with their children, in Cambridge after the colonel left. Tony became a businessman and landowner.

After the battles of Lexington and Concord, and until June 22, 1775, the house had another illustrious resident, and another colonel, also named "John". He was John Glover, head of the Marblehead Marines. He and his officers used the house for their headquarters, while most of their men pitched tents on the lawn. The Marblehead group would later help the next resident, George Washington, rowing him and his soldiers across the icy Delaware River to attack the Hessians in Trenton, New Jersey, on Christmas night, 1776. The Glover group only stayed a few weeks in the house.

George Washington, newly elected commander-in-chief, assumed command in July and, though he had headquarters at Harvard College, used the house as a residence as did General Gates. Washington used the first floor to greet guests and hold meetings. Washington's account book shows this entry: "Cash paid for clearing the House which was provided for my Quarters

& had been occupied by the Marbleh. Regimt." The amount was two pounds ten shillings and nine pence.

It was in this house that the commander gave orders to Benedict Arnold for his expedition to attack the British in Quebec after taking his troops through Maine. Here, too, Washington confronted Dr. Benjamin Church with evidence he had been given that showed Church to be a British spy rather than a patriot as supposed.

Washington dwelled in the house during the time of the Siege of Boston until the British had evacuated in the spring of 1776. In addition to its closeness to Harvard College, which was military headquarters for the colonials, the house had a splendid view of Boston. A later purchaser would ensure that this view would prevail by purchasing the land between it and the Charles River.

It was an excellent place to hold meetings, but also in which to entertain. Martha Washington joined her husband in December 1775 and stayed for four months. On January 12th, the couple celebrated their wedding anniversary with a fete in the house.

After the war, the home was purchased by Nathaniel Tracy, who had been a successful privateer under Washington, capturing several British vessels. He in turn sold it to Thomas Russell who lived there from 1786–1791 during the summers. Legend has it that Russell was so rich that one morning, for breakfast, he had a sandwich made of two slices of bread and a hundred dollar bill. He kept the house six years and then sold it to Andrew Craigie who had built the bridge near the mouth of the Charles.

Andrew Craigie, for whom the house is named, and his wife Elizabeth were the owners from that point until 1819. Andrew was the first Apothecary General of the Continental Army, serving it at Bunker Hill, Germantown, and Valley Forge where he was in charge of medical services. He made lots of money at that time.

The Puritans who lived in his neighborhood did not like the ornate enhancements that Craigie added to the house. He built an ell with a large kitchen and dining room for entertaining— which he did a lot. He also added a garden with a greenhouse and icehouse. To make the house suitable for his fancy guests, Craigie had furniture built to his specifications, had china imported, carpets woven, hung maps and prints on the walls, and built a well-stocked wine cellar.

These were not one-time things. He had so many guests that he was always importing things from England and abroad. Craigie, unmarried at that time, had many horses, chaises, and sleighs. He also had an eye for women.

Craigie gave a splendid garden party at which he broke up two engagements. A friend from Boston strolled with Craigie in his garden marveling at all that he had, but Craigie, who was walking a short distance behind two young ladies, said he was miserable because he was in love with one of those two women, but they were both engaged.

A few days later, the friend returned to tell Craigie that Miss Foster had broken her engagement and the coast was now clear for him. Craigie had to inform him that it was the other young woman with whom he was in love. In a few more days, the friend had managed to intervene in the other engagement and convince the father of Elizabeth Shaw that he should throw over the young student to whom she was engaged. He did this, and the young woman unhappily married the older, duller Craigie.

Craigie, meanwhile, entertained the rich and the powerful and secretly bought up land in east Cambridge near Lechmere's Point.

He built his bridge in 1809 and began to sell his property. But it sold slowly, even when he offered to build a county courthouse and jail there. Those didn't help much. He fell deeply into debt. The sheriff, from that same courthouse, pursued him regularly and Craigie had to hole up in his mansion on the Charles. When he died in 1819, deeply in debt, only six people attended his funeral.

His widow, Elizabeth Shaw Craigie then moved into the back of the house and leased the remaining rooms. Among her tenants were three Harvard presidents and many professors. She sat in her window wearing a long, gray cloak and white turban and read, as we've said, Voltaire.

One professor added his name to the house in due time—but he almost didn't. Henry Wadsworth Longfellow had just become Professor of Modern Languages at Harvard, but somehow he didn't look or carry himself like a professor. Mrs. Craigie thought he was no more than a student and refused at first to rent to him. Longfellow was able to convince her by showing himself to be the author of the book she was just then reading—a book not written by Voltaire. Mrs. Craigie reluctantly let him rent the rooms George Washington had occupied, and his association with the Craigie House (later the Craigie/Longfellow House) would be memorable.

When he lost his first wife, Longfellow returned to America, he began his professorship at Harvard and was required to live in Cambridge. That brought him to his rooms (or George Washington's rooms) at Craigie house in 1836

Longfellow then began to court a woman he had met in Switzerland. She was Fanny Appleton, the daughter of Beacon Hill Brahmin, Nathan Appleton, one of the founders of the textile industry and part-owner of mills at Waltham and later in Lowell. Their romance, though, was a slow starter. Longfellow proposed and Fanny turned him down. But he persisted, frequently walking to Beacon Hill by crossing the bridge to Boston. It was later replaced by a bridge from East Cambridge to near Charles Street which was later named the Longfellow Bridge.

Seven years into the courtship she wrote him a letter accepting his proposal, and his father-in-law, Nathaniel Appleton, purchased the Craigie House where Longfellow was living, as a wedding gift for his daughter and her poet husband. Appleton also bought the land between the house and the river. Longfellow was proud of the house, calling it "…the house which Washington has rendered sacred."

Longfellow wrote many of his best works while living in the house, and he and Fanny put in a formal garden, central heating, gaslights, indoor plumbing, and carpets, and furnished the house with items from Tiffany's in New York.

Longfellow became America's most popular poet and his fame spread throughout the world. Many of his best-loved works contributed to America's appreciation of their country, even to a celebration of its history. His "Midnight Ride of Paul Revere" is still fixed in many people's minds as a true account of what happened in April 1775, though parts of it are in error. There were also "The Song of Hiawatha," "The Village Blacksmith," and "Evangeline," the story of the transplanting of Acadians from Nova Scotia to Louisiana.

The couple had six children there and both parents died in the house, Longfellow in 1882. Alice, his eldest daughter, continued to live there until 1928. She was a founder of Radcliffe College.

Present location of the Craigie Bridge, built in 1910 along with the first dam and locks.

Henry Wadsworth Longfellow Dana, his grandson and the grandson of Richard Henry Dana, Jr., author of the epic *Two Years Before the Mast*, lived in the house from 1917–1950 and was the house's first curator. In 1963 the Longfellow House Trust was formed to preserve and enhance the house and grounds, and in 1972 it was made a National Historic Site. It now functions as a museum as part of the Longfellow National Park.

Fanny died tragically in 1861 from burn wounds—her dress caught fire from a lighted match or from hot wax while Longfellow slept in the next room. Hearing her screams he awakened and tried to stifle the flames with a small rug. He managed mostly to burn himself, scarring his face and leading him to wear a beard the rest of his life. Fanny died the next day. For months, Longfellow lived in continual grief and depression.

Longfellow remained in Cambridge for the rest of his life, although he spent summers at his home at Nahant. In 1868, Longfellow made his last visit to Europe with his three daughters. He spent two days with the English poet Alfred Tennyson in the Isle of Wright. Queen Victoria, who was his great admirer, invited him to tea.

With his command of twelve languages, Longfellow was also an effective translator. One of his most famous works was his translation of Dante's *Divine Comedy*. He completed that work in 1867 after many years. During that period he formed the "Dante Club" with other literary masters joining him to confer on his work. The club and its famous members, like Oliver Wendell Holmes, became the basis for a best-selling mystery novel, *The Dante Club*, by Matthew Pearl of Cambridge and Harvard.

After his death, Longfellow's reputation declined quickly, and continued to as the culture changed and his poetry was viewed by some of the intelligentsia as simplistic rhyming often perpetuating myths. However, he, like Norman Rockwell, who reflects a similar nostalgic middle-class Americana, has enjoyed something of a revival.

Longfellow was a regular member of the Saturday Club that met at the Parker House in Boston. Surprisingly, he was not the only "star." The club was made up of all the literary lights of the era who lived around Boston, as well as some who were just visiting, such as Charles Dickens. It was an intellectual group unique to its time and its place. Saturdays may never be the same again.

Land bought by Fanny Appleton's father is now Longfellow Park.

The Craigie-Longfellow House on Brattle St.

9

Not far from the Longfellow House or from Mt. Auburn Cemetery, the town of Watertown had its beginnings. The place where settlers stepped ashore after sailing up the Charles was later known as Gerry's Landing after Eldredge Gerry, whose home was nearby Elmwood.

Gerry was a signer of the Declaration of Independence, Governor of Massachusetts, and Vice President of the United States under James Madison. His name is associated with "gerrymandering," a process for drawing congressional districts to favor the party in power. Gerry's Landing is located next to the south side of today's Eliot Bridge.

Another famous name is attached to the landing of the first party of settlers in Watertown. Richard Saltonstall founded Watertown where the wide Charles narrowed, and set a pattern, though he didn't know it.

Over a period of years every bend in the river had its own settlement on both banks, founded by the restless people of previous towns, which gave birth to the next one. Accompanying Saltonstall was a minister named George Phillips. Their settlement would be called "Saltonstall Plantation."

Earlier that year, 1630, another group of Puritans spent a few days in Watertown, but did not stay. Roger Clap and some others from Dorchester had been there in May, landing on the steep banks where the Perkins Institute is located now. These men met the native Paquossettes who gave them a large bass for a meal. The Puritans, in turn, offered a biscuit. The meeting is commemorated on the town seal. The group went on to settle in Dorchester where they expected to find better pastureland. They were unlikely to find better farmland, for Watertown's was excellent. The place they encamped in Watertown was called Dorchester Fields.

Sir Richard Saltonstall, the leading planter, was part of an important English family and was able to help the colony even when he returned to England after a year. He was also an early contributor to a planting of another sort —the establishment of Harvard College. A later member of the family would be one of the more principled judges during the Salem Witchcraft Trials, and during the twentieth century, Senator Leverett Saltonstall would live farther out on the Charles in Dover.

The court in Charlestown decreed that the town on the Charles River be called "Watertown." That may have been because it was reached via water, or because it was a well-watered area. The Indian name of the town was Pigsgusset —which was not chosen. The village, though populous, was compact. Its location, six miles upriver from Boston, lies mostly parallel to the river, on the north side of it, though it used the south side of the river as well for fishing and later would acquire those areas. The spire of the church could be seen from both sides of the river just as today both Perkins School and the Arsenal buildings are visible.

In 1632, Watertown people protested against a tax levied on them without their consent for a stockade built at Cambridge. Their protest was the first in America against taxation without representation. It was a spirit and attitude that led to representative government in the Bay Colony. The Native Americans in and near Watertown were generally peaceful, but one citizen, Capt. John Oldham, who had moved there from Plymouth, was victim of an atrocity. He traded with various Indian tribes, and while trading on Block Island, he was murdered by Native Americans in a manner that outraged settlers and led to the Pequot War.

Oldham had other adventures as well.

Mt. Auburn Hospital at Gerry's Landing

Motorboat near Mt. Auburn Cemetery

Elmwood was home to Eldridge Gerry, James Russell Lowell, and others.

Elmwood, off Brattle Street, was part of Tory Row.

John Oldham is a little-known but fascinating character from the yellowing pages of history. Oldham makes it onto these pages because he played a part in Watertown history. In fact, for a time, Oldham actually lived on an island in the river. But his wild adventures were in the mold of John Smith or William Blaxton.

John was baptized at Derby, England, and a Puritan at heart—but not a Pilgrim (or Separatist), even though he came to America in 1623 to settle in Plymouth colony. He brought his wife and children as well as his sister on the voyage of the good ship *Anne* in July of that year. Captain John Oldham, as he was known, should have been a tight fit at Plymouth colony where his sister Lucretia married the son of William Brewster, a signer of the Mayflower Compact.

But troubles were brewing at Plymouth, too. A casual brush with history may not pick up the fact that more than half of those who came to America on the *Mayflower* were not Separatists like the Pilgrims who wanted to separate entirely from the Church of England. Many, in fact, came for what they thought would be an economic opportunity. The Plymouth Company had made arrangements to sell fish, furs, and timber, which they expected to be plentiful. These adventurers, for the most part, didn't care a fig about the Pilgrims' religious aspirations.

That was also true of many who came after the *Mayflower's* voyage. One of these was Rev. John Lyford, who was the first minister to come to the colony. He came on the *Charity*, and pretended to be sympathetic to the Separatists, but was a clandestine supporter of the Church of England.

Lyford gathered support from other non-Pilgrims in Plymouth, including our John Oldham. These men wanted to worship as they used to back in England, and they were meeting secretly to do so. It was dangerous when a small, imperiled colony had a divided loyalty, and the Pilgrim leaders, including Governor William Bradford, realized what was happening. He viewed Lyford and Oldham as deviants who were trying to destroy the colony and doing a good job of it.

If the Puritans had their *Scarlet Letter*, then Plymouth had Lyford's letters, and they were no fiction. The radical reverend had been corresponding with allies in England, taking potshots at the Pilgrims. Captain Oldham had been doing the same. Unfortunately for them, they drew the suspicions of Governor William Bradford who intercepted some of the letters, read them, and called Lyford and Oldham on the carpet.

Lyford apologized and said he was just reporting what he had heard, but Oldham became heated when informed that Bradford had been reading what they thought was private correspondence. He refused to fulfill his guard duty, thus provoking an argument with Miles Standish, who was in charge of the Pilgrims' military affairs. Standish had a short temper that matched his stature, and was always ready for a fight.

Oldham, too, was fiery. He pulled a knife on Standish, who'd been in knife fights before. Oldham used what must have been strong language back then, calling Standish a "beggarly rascal."

The upshot of the skirmish and the letters was that Oldham and Lyford had to undergo a trial for "plotting against them and disturbing their peace, both in respects of their civil and church state." Brotherly love did not prevail and there was no forgiveness coming. They were turned out into the cruel wilderness.

Lyford's trial was not at an end. Sarah Lyford, his wife, brought forth further charges against the randy reverend. It seems he had impregnated another woman before they married. Sarah had heard rumors, but Lyford swore an oath that they were untrue. After their marriage she learned that he had lied, and they took in his bastard child. Still he did not reform, and she could keep no maids in the household because he would have sex with them.

Nor was that the extent of Lyford's dalliances. While in ministry in Ireland he had given pre-marital counseling to a girl in his parish and raped her. When she married, her husband sensed that she had a guilty secret, and when she confessed it he got some friends and went after Lyford, who was forced to flee the country and head for Plymouth.

When Lyford and Oldham were expelled from Plymouth, about one quarter of the colonists who opposed the Pilgrims' ideas went with them. Oldham established a colony at Nantasket. Lyford went with them before moving on to Cape Ann and then to Virginia where he died. His widow remarried, moving to Hingham with her second husband, Edmund Hobart, Sr. an early settler of that town.

Oldham did better for a while. He traded with Native Americans as far south as Virginia and later spent time in England, becoming wealthy. He became overseer for shot and powder for the Massachusetts Bay Colony and moved to an island in the Charles River off Watertown, joining the church in that city. He became its representative to the General Court from 1632–34. However, he continued to trade with Native Americans from Maine to New Amsterdam (later New York).

But the peripatetic Oldham remained footloose and fancy free. He and ten others left Watertown and traveled to Connecticut, where they established the first permanent settlement in that colony at Wethersfield, south of Hartford.

His story continued a while longer, however. In July of 1636, continuing his trading forays, he was on a ship headed for Block Island off the coast of Rhode Island. His ship was boarded by hostile Native Americans, probably members of the Pequot tribe. He was killed along with five of his crew, and two young boys who were with them were captured. The ship's cargo was taken, but the two boys were rescued by a fishing vessel.

Oldham's influence lived longer than he did. When news of the Native American attack reached the Bay Colony, a force of men was sent to Block Island to retaliate.

The incident led to the Pequot War.

In anticipation of Native American raids, the general court had ordered that houses be built no farther than a half mile from the meetinghouse (in the center of town). This meant that towns and villages were rather crowded and as a result, groups of people broke away, formed new congregations in other parts of towns, or moved away entirely.

Towns were also close together, with their houses near the centers and their farms and pastures radiating out from there. These required a lot of room and, in Watertown, people felt crowded and emigrated to new settlements. The first group, as we have seen, traveled all the way to Wethersfield, Connecticut. They had gone without legislative permission. They were also religious dissenters.

Another group moved to Dedham in 1635 with permission of the General Court who decreed: "There shall be a plantation settled about two miles above the falls of the Charles River, on the northeast side thereof, to have ground lying to it on both sides of the river, both upland and meadow, to be laid out hereafter as the court shall appoint."

Watertown residents played an active part in military actions both before and during the Revolution. The town agreed not to drink the tea, which the British government was trying to foist on the colonists prior to the Boston Tea Party. On the 19th of April, when the Regulars raided Lexington and Concord, men from Watertown took part and one was killed. Subsequently, during the siege of Boston and other military actions, others died from sickness or on the field of battle.

Watertown became the focus of civic and revolutionary activity during this period. It was the location of the second and third sessions of the Provincial Congress of Massachusetts in the First Parish Church in 1775. Dr. Joseph Warren presided over it just prior to the Battle of Bunker Hill at which he was killed. The Committees of Safety and Correspondence also met in Watertown, as did the town meetings of Boston during the siege. The General Court met in Watertown (1775–78) while its committees met in the Edmund Fowle House nearby.

In the period leading up to the Revolution, the *Boston Gazette* and *Journal* was published in Boston by Edes and Gill, espousing American causes. However, its articles became outrageous to the British, and the newspaper was removed to Watertown, where it was published until the British evacuated Boston.

Watertown lost parts of its territory as populations grew and people moved farther out within the town limits. Three times, sections of Watertown were added to Cambridge, and it also gave territory to Weston, Waltham, Belmont, and Lincoln. When some of the borders were redrawn, Watertown managed to hang on to a stretch on the Newton side of the Charles, which had always been a good spot for fishing. The Native Americans and the early settlers had built weirs near the Watertown Dam, anchoring it on both sides of the river, which gave the town a viable claim at a later time.

As nearby Brighton would later do, Watertown served as a market town for cattle and horses, and also for garden products. It had built the colony's first grist mill in 1632 and similarly built one of the early woolen mills in 1662.

Industry continued in Watertown, much of it along the river. By 1837, the town had three manufactories for soap and candle products. Factories in town also made boxes, cotton, and paper.

Duck cloth and sail cloth, made of cotton, were produced in 1807 at the Bemis Factory, which actually made the sails for *Old Ironsides*. Along the river there were also factories that made chocolate, paper, dyes, and lace as well as Crawford Stoves that were sold all over the world.

But the major manufactory associated with the town and the river was the Watertown Arsenal, one of the first in the country. Its mostly brick buildings were designed by noted architect Alexander Parris, who is known chiefly for his design of Quincy Market. It served as a military munitions factory, research, and storage facility from its inception in 1816 until 1995, when the army sold the 40-acre site to the town. It played an especially key role in World War II.

The falls at Watertown made it a natural place for settlement and industry.

This placid water will churn churlishly when it cascades over the falls ahead.

A man feeds geese at the Watertown footbridge.

A goose plays "Cock-of-the-Walk" on Watertown Dam.

The former U.S. Arsenal has been adaptively reused many times.

The Arsenal area became a superfund cleanup site in the 1990s and then underwent redevelopment. It has included a retail area—the Arsenal Mall—across the street from another, the Watertown Mall, and also has housing, a health care facility, a large park, restaurants, an art center, and part of the Harvard Business School.

Farther west in Watertown Square, the Armenian Library and Museum of America holds the largest collection of its kind in North America.

The tower of the Perkins School for the Blind has stood above the Charles River in Watertown since 1912. It has a 38-acre campus, but has programs for the blind or deaf-blind and other disabilities in 65 countries around the world. However, the school was founded in 1829 in Boston, the first school of its type in the country.

The school was chartered by Dr. John Fisher who had seen the world's first school for the blind in Paris and wanted to establish one in America. He was able to get state backing through the help of powerful friends. He hired a director, Samuel Gridley Howe, who used rooms in his father's house in Boston for the classes, beginning in 1832. The school continued to gather supporters, notably the "Merchant Prince" of Boston, Thomas Handasyd Perkins, who had made a sizable fortune in the China trade. He became vice president and a trustee.

Perkins offered his home in Post Office Square for the use of the expanding school, which had by then reached more than sixty students. Perkins then sold his home and gave the money to the school for new quarters. With the money from the sale, the school bought a hotel at City Point in South Boston and named it after its benefactor.

One of Howe's goals was to provide practical training as well as academic instruction, and to this end he established a printing department to produce embossed books. He wanted to get famous authors to use the school to emboss their books, and he succeeded. Charles Dickens used Perkins School to print and distribute 250 copies of his latest book, *The Old Curiosity Shop*.

Dickens, in fact, visited the school during a lecture tour of America in 1842 during his stay in Boston; he wanted to see two things. One was the mill in Lowell with their factory girls, and the other was Laura Bridgman, who had been at the school for five years. Dickens was so impressed that he wrote a book, *American Notes*, in which he expressed his amazement at the work Howe had done with Bridgman.

One person who read the book was Kate Keller of Alabama who had a blind and deaf child of her own. She and her husband began to look for help for their daughter Helen, aged six. Their search led them first to Alexander Graham Bell, a teacher of the deaf, and then to the Perkins School, where Anne Sullivan, a graduate of the school, was chosen to go to Alabama to teach Helen. After working with the girl at home, Sullivan brought Helen to Perkins where she lived from 1888 to 1893.

The school, now world-famous, continued to grow and moved to its new building in Watertown. An addition to the school at that location was its creation of the Braille and Talking Book Library. In 1982, Perkins began to accept students with multiple disabilities beyond blindness. It also started programs for seniors who are losing their sight, and an infant-toddler program. It has recently built a new eco-friendly building on campus as it continues to prosper.

Perkins School for the Blind perches atop a Watertown hill, overlooking the Charles.

II

During the Great Migration from 1630 to 1643, swarms of Puritans left England for religious reasons, landing mostly on the shores of Massachusetts Bay, both north and south of Boston. They soon occupied many of the most desirable locations. That meant that the next group had to move inland—their route was along the Charles River.

Cambridge—or "Newtown" as it was first known— had, in fact, been deliberately chosen because of its inland location and presumed safety from attack via oceangoing ships, though it was still close to Boston.

Cambridge became a stopping off point for those who had not yet acquired a home location. As a result, the General court gave Cambridge large tracts of lands including areas as far north and west as Billerica and Bedford, much of Lexington and all of Arlington, Brighton, and Newton.

Still, Cambridge itself took until late in the next century to greatly expand its own population. What typically happened was that groups of people moved to new population centers within the town, formed their own churches and then became separate towns. New arrivals also departed for areas as distant as Connecticut.

Meanwhile, south of the Charles, the area west of Brighton that would become Newton began to fill slowly, probably because of its distance from the ocean, which was the usual source of livelihood for New Englanders. Nor did Newton have thick stands of timber or even much good farmland, so those who did come, set up near the river and raised livestock while some of the early villages depended on waterpower.

Reaching Boston was actually quite difficult, too, especially at low tide. One had to cross the mudflats or wait for the occasional ferry. Traveling the ten miles would have had to be mainly on foot, or by farm wagon, and as a result early Newtonites were mostly isolated from Boston and Newtown.

The town which had by then changed its name to Cambridge was not eager to lose any more tax revenue by having more towns "spin off" to become separate entities, and Newton's journey toward independence was slated to be a long one.

That growth was also unconventional. It occurred in spurts and in a number of different locations, which probably accounts for its present day configuration as a city composed of a dozen or so "villages" with no central downtown or main street.

That's not a description of most urban areas of the United States. It's one of the things that makes Newton unique, and it appears to have begun during the formative years when people settled wherever the geography suited them and often where the Charles River insinuated its way liquidly into their lifestyles. So it was; so it remains.

The first of those early Newton settlers to plant roots was Deacon John Jackson, who settled on Brighton Hill in 1639. That drumlin, also called Nonantum Hill, stretches between Oak Square, Brighton to near Newton Corner, and provides views of the Charles and beyond. Members of his family came next, settling their own acreage nearby. That was fairly typical as members of various families settled south of the river—and near it at first, with homes away from the river appearing later. The sparse population still had to go to church in Cambridge until the first Newton meetinghouse was built in 1660 at the corners of Cotton and the present Centre streets. The first village, at today's Centre and Washington Streets, is often called Newton Corner, but it was little more than a farming trade center among scattered farms. Cambridge showed little but contempt for Newton's efforts at self-government and rebuffed them for 25 years. In the argot of the times, the Cambridge bourgeoisie complained: "Those long-breathed petitioners rested not, but continued to bait their hooks, and cast their lines into the sea, tiring out the Courts with their eager pursuit, and obliging them to dance after their pipers for twenty-five years."

Newtonites must have been stars at dancing, because they continued to advance their cause and inexorably wore down their

Jackson House, donated by a prominent early Newton family is now the town museum. It's near Newton Corner and Nonantum.

tired opponents as well as the courts, one presumes. Curiously, one of those members of the General Court who pledged to decide the question was one Major Nathaniel Hawthorne of Salem, ancestor of the man of the same name who would become a great American novelist and who would live part of his life, 200 years hence, in Newton.

By 1688, that fight was won. Newtown (its name then) was freed by the General Court from its inclusion as part of Cambridge. Three years later it was known as Newtown, but this was modified to "Newton" by the town clerk, Judge Fuller. Its population remained small, however, reaching only 1,300 by the time of the Revolution.

12.

When John Smith explored the mouth of the Charles a number of years before William Blaxton came to the Shawmut peninsula, Smith had seen Native Americans in the area. Many of them would die in the epidemics that followed, but each time a settler traveled down the river it was clear that the remnants of the Algonquin tribe were still there.

One of the *sagamores,* or leaders, of that tribe was called "The Wind" or "The Spirit" in his native Mohican language, which was spoken by all the tribes who lived in New England. His name was Waban, and he was born in Concord. Though neither he nor his father was a chief, Waban rose to become a respected leader because of his varied gifts, and he did marry Tasunsquam, who was daughter of a chief or sachem.

Groups of young men from his tribe often traveled to the ocean, following the river from near today's Watertown Square, where he once met the Puritans from Dorchester and then Saltonstall's company. The Algonquins often stayed on the hills above the river in the summer because the mosquitoes were not so thick there, and because they could fish near the rapids of the Charles where they stretched a weir. The channel was narrow, and the salt flats, which began there, yielded abundant shellfish as well. The Algonquins showed the colonists how to use the fish they caught as fertilizer to grow corn as well, and relations remained peaceful right up to the Pequot War.

These Native Americans called the river Quinobequin, meaning circular or meandering. Even before they founded Watertown, the Puritans had settled in Charlestown, and William Blaxton had set himself up on Beacon Hill. When he'd been a hermit on the hill, living without white neighbors, Blaxton had made periodic trips to visit and trade with the Algonquins and other tribes. They had tobacco, food, and furs to offer for tools and metal trinkets. Blaxton was a minister and a man without airs who liked the simple life just as the tribes did.

One young native who became a good friend was Waban, and being an inquisitive and intelligent person, Waban probably learned some English and a lot about English customs and language. We do know that Waban spoke some English and was receptive to the ideas of John Eliot when they met around 1643 as Eliot began what might be called his "mission."

We have found no written evidence that Blaxton and Eliot ever met. But their years in Boston overlapped, and both were ministers. And you have to suppose that they would have conversed, discussed the interest that each had in the local natives, and that Blaxton would have told Eliot about Waban and how he had learned some English and was open to English customs—perhaps even to religious entreaties. This would have interested the younger Eliot who was about to devote his life to notions sprouting from this theme.

It's reasonable to believe that a conversation like that took place, and if it did it would have had significant impact. Blaxton, always a missionary in the traditional Christian way of thinking of one's calling, would have been obliged to pass on the knowledge that he had that might have helped a missionary who was about to follow in his shoes. Blaxton would leave Boston for Rhode Island and a new calling in 1635. Eliot was about to begin his mission and would find footsteps to follow—those of the hermit Blaxton.

This, then, is history by logic. It ought to have happened in this way; there is every likelihood that it did, so we may assume fairly that it did. But we have no proof, just as both men could not offer proof of the existence of God.

In any case, Waban became interested and receptive to the gospel according to Eliot and he established his tribe in Newton-on-the-Charles. Governor John Winthrop was in agreement with Eliot, who wanted to convert the tribe to Christianity. Eliot, meanwhile, had some sidesteps on the way to his calling. He took the place of Rev. Wilson in Boston, then became minister in Roxbury, whose Eliot Square is named for him.

John Smith visited the mouth of the Charles but thought it was a huge river. His maps helped settlers who came to Virginia and New England.

But in 1643, Eliot set out to talk with the Native Americans. He began by learning what he could of their language because he wanted to preach to them in their own tongue. He arranged to travel with Major Daniel Gookin, who had been appointed Commissioner to the Indians in New England. They would travel together with Governor Winthrop's blessing, and sometimes with him. Gookin would take care of civil matters that concerned the Native Americans, while Eliot taught them English, began to learn their language, and kept an eye out for opportunities for conversion.

The best opportunity appeared to come through Waban. Eliot visited the leader in his wigwam in Newton on the hill just west of Brighton's Oak Square above the street now called Nonantum. Eliot, alert as he was, spotted the possibilities quickly.

Waban's wigwam in Newton. He spoke for more than an hour, the Native Americans said they had understood all of it and afterwards Eliot gave out apples and biscuits to the children and tobacco to the men. Eliot had help from a New York Mohegan interpreter as he answered questions.

His preaching said that the word of God comes from the four winds—which was a bit of a coincidence since Waban was called "The Wind." Eliot also explained the commandments, which the natives said they understood. They then asked how to get to know Christ (which is a frequent question of Christians even today); they wanted to know if God could understand them if they prayed in their own language.

Rev. Eliot preaching to Waban and his tribe.

He realized that Waban was very bright, knew some English and could be a valuable nexus between the Puritans and his tribe. He and his companion, Gookin, talked it over and agreed that Waban had a major role to play in future relations between the settlers and the natives.

Gookin made Waban Governor of all the tribes. He was then 28 years old. Governor Winthrop made a trip up the Charles to visit Waban as well.

In 1646, Waban became the first Native American Eliot converted to Christianity, and in that same year, Eliot preached for the first time in the indigenous language in

Eliot told them that God had made us all, and offered an illustration. "There is a basket. It is made of white and black straws and many other things which I do not know; but the man who made it knows; he knows all that is in it."

The Native Americans also asked why God did not make all men good (another universal question), and such sundries as why sea water is salty and fresh water is not. At the end, the natives asked to hear more.

That led to a second session, and a third. The second lasted all afternoon and some of the listeners became emotional at hearing God's word. Waban, and many of his tribe, were so stirred that they didn't sleep that night.

Here, too, history is limited since we have no tape of the session and must rely on reported outcomes. We might suppose that Eliot had some of the skills later found among evangelicals like Billy Graham because he made remarkable progress while starting in a seemingly impossible position.

The third session had a surprise for those who attended. Just as later preachers stirred listeners to "witness" and "testify" to the truth they were bestowing, so Eliot evoked a response from Waban who arose and began to instruct his people—not in some halting and immature way, but eloquently and almost as though speaking in tongues. It must have been an astonishing moment.

After that, the converted and motivated Waban took four young boys, aged four to nine, and called on Eliot in his house to ask him to instruct them, asking the teacher to bring the word to his people, starting with the very young. In this way, Waban became a missionary arisen from the converted, and his tribe of people became the first community of Christian Native Americans in North America, leading a sober and industrious life along the banks of the Charles.

Eliot's preaching at Nonantum occurred at regular intervals and he had help from Waban and some white missionaries. Those who attended often included the governor and lieutenant governor, several magistrates, and Commissioner Gookin. They, too, were "testifying" to the authenticity of Eliot's preaching and its acceptance by the government. Sometimes the Gospel was preached at Waban's Nonantum wigwam or at the wigwam of another leader; other times they traveled to Natick by canoe for a service.

All these visitors respected Waban, and he was believed to have healing powers. Daniel Gookin, who was a prolific writer, mentioned his helpful praying during what was called "the great sickness." Gookin wrote:

> Several of them recovered, particularly WABAN, and John Thomas; the one the principal ruler, and the other a principal teacher of them, who were both extreme low, but God has in mercy raised them up; had they died, it would have been a great weakening in the work of God among them.

In fact, Gookin was instrumental at having Waban made Justice of the Peace by Governor Winthrop in 1646. Waban's example led to whole tribes of Native Americans becoming Christians and organizing churches in several locations in New England. Those in Nonantum were hard workers, they were pious, and they learned trades, cultivated lands, fished, and kept livestock.

Some rose above that state. Two were educated by the President of Harvard, and Eliot himself preached to a large group of Native Americans there. The college had their education as part of its charter and erected a building for this purpose, though only one Native American received a degree.

At Harvard, Eliot published an indigenous language primer, the first book in North America printed in the language of the Native Americans of Massachusetts. He also translated the Bible books of Genesis and Matthew into their language, and in 1664 printed at Harvard a complete translation of the Bible into the language, a work that took 17 years.

For his part, Waban made up a code of laws by which the Native Americans would be governed. They were similar to the laws of the Mass Bay Colony. Some were quite specific and spoke of cultural concerns:

"If any man shall beat his wife, his hands shall be tied behind him, and he shall be carried to the place of justice to be severely punished."

"If any shall kill their lice between their teeth, they shall pay five shillings."

When the General Court gave territory in today's Newton and Brighton to the Proprietors of Cambridge, they made the caveat that these holdings did not extend to lands that the Native Americans had used and improved.

However, Eliot still believed that some whites were having a negative effect upon his Nonantum Indians. In 1651, he arranged for them to move to South Natick, 18 miles upriver, but still on the Charles, to an area called "the Place of Halls," which was a wilderness when they moved there. Some Native Americans from Concord joined them there. The dam they built is still there, and they also set up a footbridge, three streets with house lots, a fort with a stockade, and a Meetinghouse, which also served as a school. Waban's followers planted "Friendship Trees" and lived there in peace for 24 years following agrarian pursuits, engaging in crafts, and becoming increasingly like the English settlers.

Others also left their nomadic lives and formed villages to separate themselves from their pagan and hunter-gatherer backgrounds and learn more about Christianity, leaving behind their lifestyles, clothing, and rituals. These villages were often called "praying Indian towns."

But it would not last. In 1675, other tribes banded together to make war on the English settlers in what became known as King Philip's War. Chief Philip (nee Metacomet) of the Wampanoags was decidedly not a Christian. He had said, "Why should I give up my thirty-seven gods for your one? I care no more for your religion than that button on your coat!"

Philip was also angry at the incursion of the settlers into the hunting and fishing grounds of the Native Americans, and at first the war went well for him. Many settlements were burned. Then the settlers banded together, out-organized their opponents, burned their villages and brought superior firepower to bear on them.

The war brought great suffering and death to Waban and the other "praying Indians." Philip and his cohorts hated them because they remained loyal to the English, and the English, panicky because of the other wild Native Americans, were suspect of all local indigenous populations. Some were "drafted" to fight for the English and were forced to stay within five of the fourteen "praying towns," and the General Court put the Natick Indians on Deer Island where they suffered from cold, lack of food, sickness, and death.

Despite the deaths and suffering, these Native Americans made few complaints. Some Bostonians even wanted to attack them there, and did vilify Eliot and Gookin for their defense of the defenseless Praying Indians.

Despite this opposition and unfair treatment, the Praying Indians from Deer Island played a significant role in winning the war. Two of them were sent as spies to provide information on the plans and locations of Philip's forces.

They did this well and also joined the commander of the colonial army to act as scouts and spies in the field, which they were glad to do.

A separate group of these braves, 80 in all, fought in the war, performed well, and caused the English to have second thoughts about how they had treated them during the dark days. Those at Deer Island were brought back to the mainland at Cambridge on the Charles River.

Waban and the others returned to South Natick after the war, but found that the things they had left behind were gone, including a sawmill they had built. Waban remained in Natick until his death, probably in 1685, at age eighty.

White settlers acquired the land the Native Americans owned and improved in Newton and used it to build mills. William Nahantan of the Ponkapoag tribe signed the deeds. But, by law, anyone buying land on this river bank had to agree to allow the Indians to fish there, and seine and dry their nets upon the banks.

While the Praying Indians had hoped to be assimilated within the European settlements, to a large degree that never happened. They had trouble adjusting to the institutionalization that the larger society was built upon because their own pursuits were more cooperative and relationship-driven.

Yet the Praying Indians survived even if their towns did not. Their descendants still live in eastern Massachusetts and recently had a 350th anniversary in Natick at which they were welcomed with the words:

"We are delighted to find this small tribe of Native Americans still practicing the blend of Puritan and traditional teachings that their forefathers and John Eliot evolved 350 years ago!"

Nonantum: the Bemis Mills

13

Nonantum: Our Lady Help of Christians Church

Nonantum is an Algonquin word that means "rejoicing." Farther west than the hill of the same name, the village lies along the Charles and south of it. Nonantum had other names, too. One that sounds like a cowboy moniker was "Tin Horn," but it had to have come later because it derives from the big horn that was blasted whenever workers were called to the mills.

Later, also, was "North Village" used in colonial times, and more recently, "Silver Lake," for the body of water, now filled in or paved over, that is found in the area. The "silver" part of the name may stem from its reflective sheen after the removal of layers of peat by immigrants from Ireland who burned the peat in place of coal to heat their homes as they had in Ireland.

The name changed from North Village to Nonantum only after the Nonantum Worsted Company bought the Dolby Mills on Chapel Street in the late 1860s. It provided employment for almost six hundred residents of the "North Village."

When settlement began, the area was largely a low plain that sloped in the direction of the Charles and had early farms along California and Watertown Streets, which intersect near the Watertown Dam, and farms on Crafts Street, farther south and west.

But growth came in the waning years of the 1600s with the establishment of the Bemis Mill at Bridge Street, which crosses the Charles. That began the rise of that section as a place that made cotton, woolens, and rope as well. Bemis built brick factory buildings where Silver Lake used to be along Nevada Street and east to Chapel Street. The general neighborhood bristled with rows of workers' houses, which were small, but looked even smaller against the towering smokestacks of the nearby mills.

The first paper-making on the Charles was not at Lower Falls, but at the less formidable dam at Bridge Street in Nonantum where David Bemis and Enos Sumner built the first paper mill in 1778, just as the Revolutionary War was getting into full swing.

Bemis lived until 1790, and by that time he not only had his Newton paper mill, but also snuff and gristmills on the other side of the river in Watertown. That was fortunate because Bemis had three sons. Isaac died four years later, so Luke and Seth handled the businesses. David Bemis had been more than lucky and industrious; he had been intelligent, too, or "smart" as Yankees of that day would more likely have said. He had educated his sons well, and Seth went on to graduate from Harvard. He began a career as a lawyer, but gave that up, using his acquired scientific background to do experiments and begin innovations that would promote the industrial revolution in its Boston chapter.

Seth left Luke in charge of the paper mill and bought out his brother's share of the mills on the Watertown side. There he conducted experiments in producing chocolate and working on dyes and medicinal roots. He also invented a "devil," a machine that prepared cotton before it was carded. Picking over the cotton had been done by hand, providing many hours of work for semi-skilled laborers, who subsequently lost their jobs. It also saved money for the company.

Like many successful entrepreneurs before and since, Seth understood the value of making the most of situations, even when prospects looked gloomy.

When trade embargoes and then the War of 1812 cut off the supply of manufactured goods from Great Britain, Holland, and elsewhere, he started a manufactory of cotton in Watertown where they made sheeting, shirting, ticking, and satinet (a cloth made from cotton that had a finish like satin).

Acting on the tip of a shipowner who felt the need to fill a shortage, he began to make duck cloth for sails. The word "duck" appears to be a corruption of a Dutch word *zeildoek*, which means "sailcloth." It is composed of two words, *zeil* meaning and sounding like "sail," and *doek* for "cloth." Holland supplied much of the sailcloth, a heavy fabric used for cotton canvas and called duck in America.

Bemis worked with a knowledgeable Englishman in extracting gas from coal. He used the gas to light his Watertown factory—first in 1812. Visitors, many of them foreign, came to see his factory, which was illuminated two years before a similar process was used in England. Alas, the gas leaked out of the jerry-built tin pipes and could no longer be used.

Next (1821) came the paper mill. Seth bought it from Luke and built a rolling stone dam, a unique invention, duplicated only once anywhere—near Warwick Castle in England. The dam was controlled by a drum that could be rolled up and down the face of the dam. The only trouble was, when it was built, it brought woes to the nearby and upstream Boston Manufacturing Company in Waltham.

They complained that the new dam was backing up the river to the point where it kept their waterwheels from turning properly. Francis Cabot Lowell and the Boston Associates offered to pay Bemis $1,000 an inch to lower his dam. He lowered it by a foot. However, the Waltham Associates soon moved to the Merrimack Valley because they needed more power than the Charles could provide.

The Bemis mills continued into the late 1840s with Seth, his brother Luke, and later Seth Jr. running all the mills on both sides of the river. In 1840, Seth sold the dye works to William Freeman, and a decade later his son sold the textile mill to the same man. When the dye works closed, a wire rope was attached to waterwheels on both sides of the river, to give more power to the mills in Watertown. Freeman was one of the principles who incorporated Aetna Mills on the corner of Bridge Street & Pleasant Street. (It is currently the home of Boston Scientific.) Buildings remain on both sides of the river.

The rolling stone dam was breached in later years and the breach remains, allowing passage for fish and for small craft like kayaks.

The Bemis Mill on the Watertown side

The Bemis Mill in Nonantum, now Meredith Instruments

14.

All this manufacturing required workers, and in the middle-to-late 1800s and beyond that meant immigrant workers. The Irish came first to Newton. The men began mostly building houses, for which Nonantum had a need, and the women worked mostly as domestics.

French-Canadians came in a significant wave in the 1880s and they worked largely in the mills. The Italians were the third wave, and in many ways they would have the most lasting influence on the area. Many of them found work on the roads and on the railroad as well as in the mills.

Jews arrived from many Eastern European countries where they had been subjected to persecution from pogroms in Russia, the Ukraine, and parts of the old Austro-Hungarian empire. They established a synagogue on Adams Street, which continues to be active. Nonantum became the most densely populated part of Newton with a polyglot of religious and ethnic populations, and eventually developed its own character.

These immigrant groups occupied the low-cost housing on its small lots that we have mentioned. Curiously, the choice of housing reflected the hierarchy within the mills. Foremen and the top-skilled workers had two-family homes built for them, while those with lower positions and lesser skills had to reside in rented rooms or in boarding houses.

The "tin horn" could be heard in these residential areas, and it was to the advantage of the employees and to the factories to have their workers close at hand and at ready call in the clustered housing between Bridge and Chapel Streets, extending well to the south in this sector. Much of the housing, or its predecessors—through the adaptive reuse of the same buildings—remain today in this closely-knit neighborhood.

This was not a suburban setting. Nonantum, unlike most of Newton, looked more like a neighborhood of Boston, Worcester, or Providence than like most of the "Garden City," though it retained some of its rural features. Nonantum had its local shops, social clubs, churches, and civic bonding. That may be illustrated by the dominant Italian sub-culture that still marks the area as it did in the 1800s.

This neighborhood is a good example of how an agricultural community changes to a modern one as advances are made in technology, transportation, and with an influx of immigrant groups. Still standing is a row of houses on Bridge Street that are representative of those built during the late nineteenth century and used by mill workers.

Nonantum's most prominent family, the Bemises, once lived at 47 Bridge Street, which is still there, and the company itself owned the buildings next to the river, which remain a good example of a riverside factory building of the period.

The river was slowed by the dam, then flowed into the basement level of the mill where its power turned huge wheels that were connected by a series of gears and shafts to equipment upstairs. The mill pond behind the dam insured that plentiful water was on hand to keep things moving.

Remnants of the dam remain, including two arches next to the mill that allowed the water to flow through.

The Nonantum Worsted plant that gave the area its name is echoed in the large Chapel Bridge Park development that occupies most of the space between California and Watertown Streets. The plant continued to operate after World War II. It was originally a hosiery mill built by Thomas Darby, an Englishman who sold it to the even larger Nonantum Worsted after the civil war, which hired hundreds of people to run its textile machines.

A striking anomaly of the Nonantum culture is "Lake Talk." This is an argot or idiosyncratic patois spoken in the village, especially among its Italian-American members. It appears to be a blend of Italian and a kind of group-code that stems from World War II when many Americans fought in Italy, and many Italians came to the U.S. The "Lake" in the name comes from the Silver Lake district based on the phantom lake of erstwhile years. Some experts say it has similarities to Italian Romany, a kind of gypsy slang, especially since many in the village descend from the same area—Donato Val di Comino, Italy. Some of the phrasings have found their way into what might be called "Boston Speak" with terms such as *wicked pissa*.

Massachusetts State Auditor Joe DeNucci, a Nonantum native, told the Boston Globe: "You talk the Lake language and only people from there can understand you. An awful lot of what it means is how you say it and how you use it. You improvise a lot, mixing it with carnival talk and bebop."

This comes from someone, whom in his neighborhood, might be called a *wicked pissa*, *mush*, or "extremely awesome guy."

Signs of the vanished Silver Lake remain in Nonantum.

15

The rapid growth of the Newton villages in the northern part of town began in parallel with the growth of traffic along today's Washington Street. That street was the route to Boston from western settlements, and it made Newton Corner the town's first village. It was a "Corner" in the sense that the road from Brighton had to turn a corner to get to Washington Street or to reach Galen Street and head for Watertown. Similarly, Centre Street from Newton Centre had to pass through a sort of triangle to reach those streets. Washington Street from the west did not continue in a straight line into Brighton Road.

The key development was the coming of the railroad in 1834. Its train was called the Meteor, and it chugged along at a breathtaking six miles an hour—which was enough to foment suburban growth, especially in the northern part of Newton, a growth that continued steadily for more than 100 years. The railroad, too, would parallel Washington Street from the west, and at Newton Corner it would veer toward the river and the Faneuil section of Brighton.

Newton Corner and the hills around it thus became attractive to wealthy Bostonians who wanted suburban retreats away from the stultifying air of the city. While many of them kept their townhouses, they used their country estates on weekends and especially during the summer.

They weren't the only ones. Daily transportation made it possible for ordinary tradesmen and shopkeepers to live in Newton and commute to Boston. Real estate became more valuable close to the train station and homes also began to appear on streets more distant from the line of the Boston & Worcester. This growth took hold especially after the Civil War in the way that boom periods so typically follow wars. In 1870, the ancestor of the Newton Free Library opened on Centre Street south of the Corner. A public library is one of those civic institutions that indicate that the town and the people living there are quite serious about staying. Firehouses are another.

The main line of the railroad extended west along the same axis as today's Washington Street. Later the Massachusetts Turnpike Extension was built on its right of way and in essentially the same place. Both of those spurs brought population growth, but provided a physical division in the community, the Turnpike's barrier coming in the form of a trench.

Newton Corner at Galen and Washington Streets near the Mass. Turnpike

This park near Newton Corner makes a quiet setting across from senior housing.

16

The Washington Street corridor was also the path of most growth, and Newtonville was another village that sprang up post Civil War like a bud on a branch. Commuter trains reached it nearly as quickly as they reached Newton Corner, and its daily commuters included businessmen, tradesmen, and professionals. They lived in modest, wood frame buildings on large lots as well as some larger homes.

There were also farms remaining from earlier times, one of them belonging to the Fullers. Judge Abraham Fuller was a gruff-speaking citizen from the Revolutionary era, who served the town and the Commonwealth well. His son-in-law General William Hull, who fought in the War of 1812, enlarged the farmhouse where Newton North High School later had its athletic fields.

The agricultural nature of Newtonville gave way in the 1840s to suburban development similar to that of Newton Corner and West Newton, as real estate developers saw the value of its proximity to the railroad.

West Newton, too, was a tiny farming community with only a scattering of buildings along that same Washington Street. Some parts remained covered with trees and swamps and marshland that reached the Charles and north beyond that to Waltham. But in Puritan times West Newton established a second parish. A dispute arose over the parish's boundary and the decision was made by drawing a line through a squash field. Detractors, who lived in the rival Newton Centre, called West Newton "Squash End." Nonetheless, town hall was moved to West Newton from Newton Centre in 1848, where it stayed until the 1930s.

Like Newton and Newtonville, West Newton grew because of the railroad, particularly after the Civil War. That meant an upsurge in real estate and new construction. Larger homes appeared on West Newton Hill while day laborers and Irish immigrants lived close to the river and the Waltham border.

Development grew even more after mid-century when the Charles River Railroad was built. The railroad is best known for serving the Upper Falls and for its use in transporting gravel fill from East Needham to Back Bay when that area of the Charles was being filled in during the 1860s and '70s.

As the line was improved though, it brought regular commuter service to Newton Centre, adding population there because the line connected to Boston.

In 1886, a commuter loop known as "The Circuit" and later as the "Highland Branch" began service from Boston through Brookline, first as far as Newton Highlands and then northwest to Riverside where it connected with the main line. The Highland Branch was a two-track line, while the Main Line had four tracks and ran from Riverside along Washington Street to Brighton and Boston. Up to 35 trains a day traveled the Circuit.

The railroad had been built to serve the industries at Newton Upper Falls, and commuter trains ran infrequently at first, discouraging development. This was especially true during the 1860s, when trains operated around the clock transporting gravel for the filling of Boston's Back Bay, an immense project that lasted more than a decade.

Waban, a village named for the Native American chief who had lived on Nonantum Hill near the river, became a station stop on the highland line. It is believed that Waban and his tribesmen often hunted near today's village. Its development came later than villages along the river, the first residents being the Woodwards whose descendants have lived there for years, their homestead having been made a National Historic Landmark Preservation Site.

The village had many large farms along Beacon Street and Woodward Street, and a decade after the Civil War, all the land in the area was held by 20 or so farmers. But as developers bought tracts along the Highland Branch, new streets with house lots formed the nucleus of suburban development.

Newton Highlands, also inland from the river, didn't really get going until the railroad did. It was just a sleepy village in

Villages have sprung up along Washington Street since early times, like this one at West Newton.

Waban Village, Beacon St., Newton

Newton Centre is graced by this late nineteenth-century Romanesque style building which now houses businesses.

colonial days served by Dedham Street running north-south and Beacon Street running east-west. The agricultural period for Newton Highlands lasted well past the Civil War.

The railroad had been built for the industry at the Upper Falls, and there was little service for passengers, so development did not follow. Trains ran completely around the clock for more than a decade, and so they, and the line, were tied up with gravel travel. But once that task was completed, and the Back Bay filled, commuter rail was available and growth began so that by 1874 Newton Highlands was established with more than 500 residents, many from Boston.

The Highland Branch of the railroad also stimulated development around the Newton Centre and Eliot stations, as well as at Chestnut Hill in the southeast. The depots along both sides of the Circuit were designed by Henry Hobson Richardson whose best-known work is Trinity Church in Copley Square. One of his last designs was Waban station, finished in 1886, a few years after his death. It had a slate roof and its walls were made of pink granite, but sadly, like all but one of them (Woodland Station), it has been demolished.

In all, Richardson designed nine stations for the Boston & Albany and, after his death, others were designed in his style—more than twenty of them—by the architectural firm of Shepley, Rutan, and Cooledge, all of whom had worked for him. Many stations were landscaped by Richardson's colleague, Frederick Law Olmsted, the great American landscape architect.

Some of the Richardson stations have been converted to other uses; two in Newton designed by the architectural firm serve as green line stations for the MBTA.

Among the Highland Branch station stops, the farthest east among the Newtons is Chestnut Hill. The area was founded by the Hammond family in 1665 and they owned a prodigious amount of property—all of Chestnut Hill that is now in Newton, including Hammond Woods, Hammond Pond, and of course Hammond Street. They and their relatives had it largely to themselves for the longest time. Joseph Lee of Beverly bought the Hammonds' farm in 1822 and was among only a few people who lived in the area. He had six nieces and nephews who were his

heirs. They had ideas and plans for development. The area would become a community of large estates called Chestnut Hill.

It wasn't easy to reach Hammond Street and its environs until long after much of Newton had already begun its development. When Beacon Street was extended through Brookline to Newton in 1850, and when the Charles River RR was built two years later, that changed. The improved rail service brought more of the Lee family from Essex County as well as their friends and associates. These included families like the Lowells, Cabots, Lawrences, and Saltonstalls. It has been referred to as the "Essex Colony."

They were sort of a "beachhead" for the mild invasion that would follow, but not until the 1880s when good transportation took hold. During the next thirty years the land that was not occupied was divided into large building lots, a farm and some private estates. A lot of the homes were Georgian, others Colonial Revival or Shingle style. There were also a goodly number of chestnut trees from which the area took its name.

The latest of the villages to develop was Oak Hill, in the southern part near Brookline and West Roxbury. It was built after World War II mostly to provide housing for returning servicemen. It was financed by the city and largely self-contained.

Newton Centre: The First Baptist Church in Newton is a National Landmark.

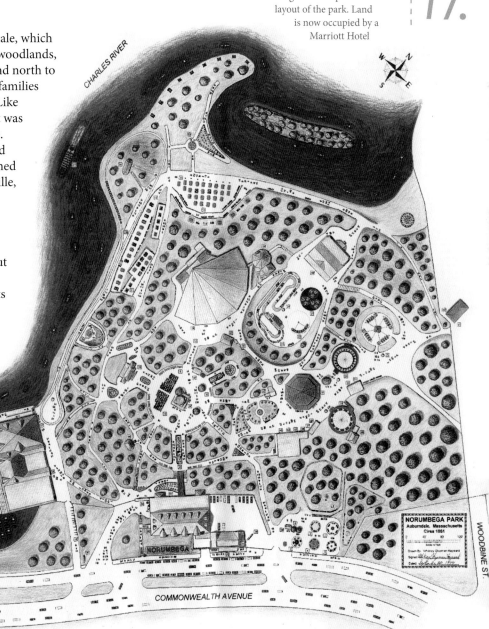

Norumbega: This map shows the layout of the park. Land is now occupied by a Marriott Hotel

The most western part of Newton is Auburndale, which began as an area of farms, rolling hills with woodlands, and marshes, especially along the Charles and north to adjacent Waltham. By the 1830s only seven families owned land there, and they owned all of it. Like other parts of Newton, that was a temporary thing, and it was the railroad that served as the catalyst for greatest change.

When passenger service was added to the Boston and Worcester Railroad, development quickly ensued. It reached Auburndale in 1837. Just as in Newton Corner, Newtonville, and West Newton, real estate speculators realized this was prime territory. A company structured to snatch up suburban commuters and entice them to invest in their properties—the North Auburndale Land Company of William Jackson—presented opportunities as they laid out streets to the north of the thoroughfare known then and now as Auburn Street, a highway, and other developments south of there.

Besides its railroad terminal, Auburndale offered a riverfront location and the recreation it could, and would, provide. The Charles offered boating, skating, canoeing, and—beyond that—Norumbega Park, whose establishment brought a huge increase in activity to the river.

This all started in the 1890s when the Newton Street Railway opened the park, twenty-one acres of recreation, a restaurant, concert hall, and canoeing areas. In the 1930s and 1940s, the Totem Pole Lounge featured the sound of the Big Bands, and you could get there from Boston by streetcar. Norumbega became a very successful family playground.

Norumbega Park was established in 1897 as a "trolley park." That meant it was set up in order to draw customers to the park via the trolley line that ran from Lake Street at Boston College, and out along the middle of Commonwealth Ave (or "Comm Ave" as people from Boston and Newton call it) to the new amusement park. The railway line was known as the Commonwealth Avenue Street Railway and billed as "Newton's, Crown of Beauty," but the park did more business than the trolley line. You could buy one ticket that included the park, the rides, and the trolley fare.

The name of the park came from Norumbega Tower, a huge stone structure standing across the Charles River at the confluence of Stony Brook, the border between Weston and Waltham. It was built to honor a supposed visit up the Charles River by the Vikings in 1000 A.D.

Evidence for such a visit is sparse, though the Vikings may have visited the present Atlantic Provinces of Canada at that time. A Cambridge professor-turned-businessman, Eben Horsford, a Harvard professor of chemistry who had invented a successful baking powder, theorized that the Vikings had been in the area, and even dug up a few artifacts near his home not far from Gerry's Landing in Cambridge to prove it. He published his findings and produced a book on his theories and enjoyed some popular support at the time, but his claims have been largely dismissed by historians and archeologists. Horsford also commissioned a statue of Leif Erickson, erected in 1887 on the esplanade of Commonwealth Avenue in the Back Bay. It has stood longer than his theories.

When the park named for the tower in Weston opened, it drew 12,000 people on its first day. It featured canoeing, picnic areas, an outdoor theatre, a zoo, penny arcade, carousel, electric fountain, and a restaurant called the Pavilion, which was run by a former slave, Joseph Lee. Lee had earlier been successful as a hotelier, running the exclusive Woodland Park Hotel in Auburndale.

Norumbega: This poster conveys a feeling of fun and outdoor activity—just as it was for many years.

The park itself was extremely successful for decades, bringing hundreds of thousands of people a year for many years. Not all of them took the trolley, however. Since the park was on the river, people came by canoe as well, and the stretch of river from nearby Riverside Recreation Grounds in Weston to other canoe rental spots in Newton and Waltham—about six miles, could boast more than 5,000 canoes, many of them emanating from a dozen boat rental areas. In the early years of the twentieth century, this area had more canoes than any other place in the world.

Some young men owned their own canoes, and this was like a teenager of the 1950s with his own car. In those days, "cruising" was done in a canoe. In fact, from 1903–05, thirty-seven couples were arrested for kissing in a canoe. This Victorian strictness was bad for business, and for a while the Newton area lost customers to the Dedham part of the Charles.

A writer in the Boston Transcript called *Chamberlain* wrote of the area:

> It is to be doubted whether any other large city in the civilized world has, within easy access to its heated human masses, a reach of river at once so attractive and so quiet as the Charles River between Waltham and Newton Lower Falls. The entire river has its delights, but below the dam at Watertown the navigator is subject to the exigencies of the tide, and, moreover, the shores are not of the wooded sort that the boatman loves to see as he floats along. Beginning at the watch works at Waltham, there is a stretch of river four or five miles long, taking in the windings, that is without rival anywhere for pleasure-boating purposes; a deep, clear river, with shores lined everywhere with vegetation. Riverside commands the whole stretch, and it is there that the excursionist from the city leaves the train and gets his boat.
>
> Below Riverside the river is entirely placid, and the low woods and thickets everywhere touch the stream, except where an occasional residence reveals a bit of lawn. Above Riverside there is a little more of wildness, with here and there a fallen trunk, over which luxuriant vegetation has scrambled, jutting into the stream, and making incomparable nooks of shade, in which our boating parties seem to have a strong and perfectly natural propensity for mooring their boats while they read or dream. Here, too, the current flows more rapidly, making navigation a bit more interesting, though it is still perfectly safe.
>
> Above the Newton Falls there is still more of lovely river, and through Dedham there are river views quite as beautiful as anything in this stretch which borders Newton, Waltham, West Newton, and Wellesley; but the Charles there is scarcely so easily accessible as it is at Riverside, and this strip will probably always be what the Seine at Bougival is to the Parisians, and the Thames from Putney to Mortlake to the English. And, compared with these hilarious resorts abroad, what a placid home of quiet respectability, the Charles is!

Norumbega, along with the Riverside Recreation Grounds in Weston and more than a dozen other local recreational facilities in Newton and Waltham, became famous for recreation, competition, romance, and fun. Riverside, just a short distance farther up the river had a swimming pool and it had the Newton Boat Club and the Boston Canoe Club, each in a clubhouse of its own. The latter was located on top of a hill on the west side of the river. It had a broad veranda with a long view of the river, and a great room with pictures and trophies and a huge brick fireplace.

Riverside was also at the connecting point of the two branches of the railroad that ran through opposite sides of Newton into Allston-Brighton on one hand and Brookline on the other.

By 1905, that outdoor theater at Norumbega had been enclosed. It held vaudeville shows, plays, and even used Mr. Edison's new invention to show moving pictures. Known as the Great Steel Theatre, it was the largest in New England, just as the zoo was the largest zoo.

As time went on, new attractions and rides appeared at Norumbega, including the Caterpillar, Dodgems, the Bug, and a large Ferris wheel. In the year 1930, the trolleys disappeared in favor of buses, and in that same year the theatre disappeared as it was converted into the Totem Pole Ballroom, which is probably remembered even more than the park itself.

The Boston area already had more than a hundred ballrooms at that time, but the Totem Pole rose above the rest. It was elegant, catered to people on their best behavior, and brought the very best in entertainment to the people of Greater Boston. Practically all the swing bands in the country performed there. When they came to the Boston area, the Totem Pole was the most likely venue. There were Benny Goodman, Artie Shaw, both Dorseys, Harry James, and later Lawrence Welk.

The famous singers were there, too. Frank Sinatra, Dinah Shore, the Four Lads, and the von Trapp singers. The bands and the singers were broadcast nationally over radio outlets, too.

The famous ballroom became a preferred destination for young couples on dates. When it was taken over by Roy Gill, in 1938, he made it non-alcoholic, instituted a dress code, and limited it to couples only. Young couples would come to the ballroom, dance on its floor, sit at tables with soft drinks, and watch the floor show. Even their parents were comfortable with the arrangement.

During World War II, an army ordinance company was located at the restaurant in the park and many war bond drives and charity events were held there. The ball field even had a professional women's softball team, the Totem Pole Belles.

The park and the ballroom occupied 21 acres in Auburndale up against the river with its canoes and paddleboats. The park's beautiful plantings and shady places were accessible to those using the ballroom, so they worked well together. Public transportation and boat rides did well during the war when automobile use was limited by rationing of gasoline and the difficulty of getting tires and parts, but after the war an automobile boom provided more opportunities for recreation and

entertainment, so both the park and the ballroom began declines that lasted until 1963–64 when both closed.

Route 128, opened in 1951, runs parallel to the Charles just across the river from Norumbega. The Massachusetts Turnpike Extension was built in 1962 and runs through Auburndale. The interchange ramp for the Turnpike is located close to where the Riverside Recreation Area used to be, and the old Riverside Station of the B&A Railroad has given way to the Riverside T station on Grove Street, somewhat north of the old depot. It is the terminus for the D branch of the T's Green Line.

The land where Norumbega Park stood is conservation land. The Marriott Hotel is located where the Totem Pole Ballroom was, and the hotel's ten acres of parking are on conservation land. If you would like a "Then and Now" look at this part of Charles River history, you might visit the Newton Historical Museum, which has an exhibition called, "Norumbega: Romance and Recreation by the River, illustrated with photos, post cards, handbills, and other artifacts. Those who lived through those times may also consult their memories.

From here to the Moody Street Dam in Waltham is the "lakes district" of the river. Many islands break the stream into inlets and coves such as Purgatory Cove, named for the baptism by immersion conducted here by the Puritans. It remains a pristine area if you can ignore the traffic drone from Route 128 west of the river. Large stretches of the banks are wooded except where a few housing areas have been built back from the coves, and until reaching the Waltham Watch Factory buildings which are being rehabilitated on the east bank near Prospect and across from the pastoral Mt. Peake Cemetery.

Charles River Boathouse rents colorful canoes and kayaks and dates to Norubega days.

A silent stretch in the Lakes Region between Newton and Waltham.

Long view of the Lakes Region, once clogged with canoes.

Heading north from the Norumbega area.

A fisherman has this cove in the Lakes Region all to himself.

Norumbega was once jammed with canoes, and still has many in bright colors.

Auburndale can post claim to a pair of identical and inseparable twins whose inventions helped improve photography and made giant strides in the automobile business. The twins were Francis Edgar and Freelan Oscar Stanley, sometimes called "F.E." and "F.O.", and they came to Newton from Maine. They had complementary skills, since F.E. had apparently inherited a gene for invention, while F.O. was an excellent manager of financial affairs and a promoter of their enterprises. That was an ideal pairing, particularly since the twins fully understood one another and could even anticipate what the other would do next.

In Maine they had made original violins, produced charcoal portraits, and taught school. They also advanced photography with their invention of an airbrush and a dry plate coating process. When they moved to Boston and then to Newton in 1890, they bought a building so that they could continue making their dry plates and photographic supplies. The dry plate earned them a lot of money when they later sold it to George Eastman, founder of Kodak. This gave the Stanleys money to spend on another invention.

The 1890s were the early years of automobile manufacturing. Some were run on gasoline or electricity, but early inventors didn't know that would be the outcome. Like Edison and his electric light bulb, which eventually glowed with a certain kind of filament, other options were tried. One was steam.

Electric cars had little power and couldn't go far. Internal combustion engines fueled by gasoline were noisy and unreliable. When you wanted to start them you had to get out front and crank the engine, and if they stalled out as they frequently did every few blocks, you had to do it again.

Steam was a natural possibility. It had driven other means of transportation such as boats and trains. Why not use it to power automobiles? In all, 125 inventors tried to come up with a steam-driven automobile, but only the Stanleys had any success. They made the effort quite on a lark. They had seen a race at a local fairground that had a small, steam car in it. It was homemade and primitive and did not by itself impress them. But it did inspire these mechanical geniuses to go it one better and make their own car.

The Stanley engine had only thirteen moving parts, so it was lighter, quieter, and faster than anything else. Once you had started it, it made steam on demand and all you had to do was watch the water level the way later drivers would watch the gas gauge. You just set the throttle and steered with the tiller.

Their quiet smoothness contrasted sharply with internal combustion (gasoline) cars that were hard to start and shift, often conked out, and were laughingly known for banging, clattering, smelling of gasoline, and frightening horses. However, steam engines took a long time to start because the steam boiler had to be brought to the right pressure, and it could take 30 minutes to get it right.

Within a year, a Stanley-made car with a chain drive and a steam engine was chugging up and down the streets of Newton—a prototype only, for the brothers kept improving on their early models. One thing they understood as mechanical engineers was that the speed of their vehicle could be enhanced by making the body lighter, and later, being from Newton, they made a racing car body from a wood and canvas canoe.

Canoes were big in Newton, especially at Riverside and Norumbega on the Charles where the river was practically clogged with them. The canoe was America's #1 recreation vehicle of its day, and the Robinson company on the Charles (near today's Route 128) made some of the best ones.

The Stanleys' cars got better and they got faster, and they soon built something else—a reputation. In 1898, they decided to mass-produce thirty of their cars. They ordered bodies from a carriage shop, but they were totally unsatisfactory to the perfectionist brothers so they decided to build their own. During the next two years they sold 200 cars—more than any other company.

Stanley Steamer, 1908 K Raceabout

Their methods would mystify today's car owners. If you wanted to buy a Stanley, you had to write to the brothers and tell them so. When your car was ready they would write back and tell you it was ready. One of the brothers would take you on the road to show you the tricks of driving a Stanley. The car cost $750, and if you weren't satisfied you just returned the car and got your money back. They didn't produce a new product line each year. The brothers made improvements so fast that each successive car was new and improved.

They then sold their car rights to a New York company for a quarter million dollars. At that point they drove one of their cars to the top of Mt. Washington—the first car to make the climb. This made the Stanley Steamer world famous. However, they had agreed not to make cars for two years. The New York company had called their own car the Locomobile, but decided it was a crazy idea and sold it back to the Stanleys cheaply. They now called their company the Stanley Motor Carriage Company.

The changes they made in their car were all innovative and they eliminated moving parts and things that would slow them down. Their new car would carry two adults and two children and would easily reach 35 m.p.h. They built 400 of them in 1902, their first production year. The twins enjoyed racing each other over the streets of Newton and nearby towns. The police often became confused over which twin they were chasing since they looked exactly the same and had the same mannerisms.

They built their runabout car for a while but they were more interested in building a fast car so they built bigger and more powerful cars to enter in races on tracks and in hill climbs to gain publicity.

They were helped in their quest by a skilled driver named Fred Marriott, and Marriott proved to be a gem. He joined the Stanleys in 1904 and became famous as a racer of steam cars. The Stanleys had made a name for themselves and their car in track meets and on climbs. Those were on Mt. Washington, at Giants' Despair Hill Club in Pennsylvania, in Britain, and in Florida.

For his part, Fred Marriott set a world record at Ormond Beach, Florida, in 1906 by racing 127+ m.p.h. Fred was sitting in a modified and inverted canoe made by John R. Robertson. Called the "Wogglebug" for a talking insect that appeared in L. Frank Baum's *The Marvelous Land of Oz*, it was made of plywood, but the top was an upside down canoe, with a space for the driver carved out.

From our distant viewpoint, a canoe made of wooden ribs covered with canvas is likely to seem antique and musty, but in 1906, the craftsmanship was actually top of the line and ahead of everything else. It was tight, taut, strong, and lightweight. Its streamlined design also was aerodynamically efficient. They even used wind tunnel testing.

The Stanleys' background brought this concept home to them before it was clear to others, although Waban and his fellow tribesmen would probably have figured it out. The Stanleys tried a number of canoes, but Robertson's suited them best and they could get the best possible design to fit their use since the factory was close at hand.

Marriott returned in 1907 to improve on his speed record. He was blazing along the track at 150+ m.p.h. when his Stanley hit a rut. The boiler flew down the track, steam jetting out of the back of it, prompting people to call the car the Flying Teapot. Marriott was seriously injured and the Stanleys gave up racing.

Marriott's mark for the steam land speed record, which had become the longest-standing such record, was finally broken more than 100 years later in August 2009 by a British racer at Daytona Beach. As for Robertson, back in Auburndale, his business was in for a decline, ironically, because the automobile replaced the canoe as a recreational vehicle, particularly for young people who wanted to be alone. The production of the Stanleys continued until 1924.

When Robertson died, his wish of having his ashes scattered over the Charles was carried out. His factory became a manufactory of tools, instruments, and transformers—Newtron Co.

F.E. always liked to drive too fast and in 1918 he died in a collision near Newburyport. F.O. moved to Colorado to help the tuberculosis he had contracted. There he built the Stanley Hotel in Estes Park in the mountains, serviced by Stanley steam vehicles, including the Mountain Wagon. (It was later associated with Stephen King's novel *The Shining*.) F.O. died in 1940. He was 91.

Another Newton product of some note is the Fig Newton®, created by Charles Roser, a baker from Ohio who sold it to the Kennedy Biscuit Works, who later became Nabisco.

The Fig Newton is a soft cookie filled with fig jam. In 1891, James Mitchell invented a machine that mass-produced them. The cookie was not named for the English physicist, as supposed by some, but for the town of Newton on the Charles. Kennedy Biscuits had a tradition of naming its products for nearby towns.

The town of Waltham was incorporated in 1738 after having been the westerly precinct of Watertown for more than a century. In fact, Waltham had to buy a meetinghouse from Newton since it didn't have one. It was purchased in 1722 and set up on Lyman Street. Once that happened, the farmers argued for and got their separation from the parent town, though there were only about 550 of them, mostly settled around Trapelo Road and Beaver Street.

Main Street (now Route 20) was part of the main highway between Boston and New York, also known as the Boston Post Road. It carried large amounts of trade, had stagecoach stops and taverns, including the Central House which was located where the library is now.

The main west-east flow of the Charles River parallels Main Street and had a dam below the Moody Street Bridge. The dam, built in 1814 to power cotton mills, created a 200-acre millpond and numerous bays and outlets in what was called the "Lakes District" part of the watershed, which reached as far south as Newton Lower Falls. The district included the Norumbega part of Auburndale, which became known for its recreational boating in the early twentieth century. It had boathouses, canoe rentals and two steamboats that made cruises up and down the district.

Moody Street was the center of the industry associated with the dam. It remains an important street, meeting Main Street at the center of town.

It is named for Paul Moody who was a key figure in the success of the American Manufacturing Company, which began the industrial binge in Waltham and later in Lowell.

Moody was born in the northern Massachusetts community of Byfield, had a limited education, and became an expert weaver in Amesbury where he made carding machinery. Next, he went into partnership to start a satinet factory.

But he arrived in Waltham just as the Moody Street Dam had begun to change things there. He had been hired by Francis

Central Square Waltham where Moody and Main Streets meet

Landry Park and the Museum of Industry and Innovation.

83

Cabot Lowell and the Boston Associates to set up machinery for their new integrated mill that would perform all the functions in making cotton, each on a separate floor of the huge factory they were building on the banks of the Charles (one that still stands as housing).

The group "Boston Associates" was comprised of the investors Lowell, Nathan Appleton, Patrick Jackson, Amos Lawrence, and Abbott Lawrence. They were all Beacon Hill Brahmins and most were related at least by marriage. They also owned most of the textile mills in Massachusetts, New Hampshire, and Maine and made about 20% of all the textiles in the country

Their textiles were mostly from plantation-grown cotton, which gave them grief later from abolitionists. However, they made big profits and invested in railroads, which they then used to carry cotton and cotton goods. They also became bankers and owned insurance companies, too. From their investments they hired thousands of workers.

F.C. Lowell was the brains behind this operation as well as a major financial backer. He had been in England a few years prior and had memorized the plans for power looms they were using. It was illegal to remove the machinery from Britain or even to take out drawings of the technology, so he found another way, and his Boston Manufacturing Company would mark the start of the industrial revolution in America.

The finished cotton was transported to Boston via a circuitous route. It was taken up Moody Street to the Boston Post Road, across Beaver Brook into Watertown, over the bridge near Watertown Square into Newton, then east at Newton Corner to Brighton Center, and south on Washington Street to Brookline Village. From there it traveled to Roxbury, past the Parting Stone at Roxbury Crossing, up hill to Eliot Square, then east and over the Neck into Boston. Only one store in Boston sold American-made cloth. That was Bowers on Washington Street.

Part of the success at Waltham was due to Paul Moody, who was a mechanical genius. The first power loom was installed under his direction, and he also improved the technology, which was rather crude and inconsistent until he made it run smoothly.

Later, in 1829, Moody patented a machine called a filling frame which helped to lower the cost of making cotton. When the company began its Lowell operation on the banks of the Merrimack River, Moody remained in Waltham but was responsible for producing the machinery, turbines, and the means of transmitting water power in Lowell. Then he moved to Lowell and became the head machinist. He developed a belting and pulley system that was used everywhere from then on for power transmission. It smoothed and leveled the operation until running the machinery no longer shook the factory with a riotous clatter of noise and vibration. It also saved time and energy. A street in Lowell was also named for him, but was later renamed.

These falls at Moody Street powered the beginnings of the textile industry in Massachusetts.

Nearby, along the river and across from the railroad tracks are the buildings that once housed the American Waltham Watch Company. It had its beginnings in Roxbury and later moved to Waltham.

The prime mover was Aaron Dennison who had seen the use of interchangeable parts in the Springfield Armory when they put weapons together. His own mass production techniques didn't catch on until the Civil War, which created a demand for inexpensive watches.

The original proprietors, Davis, Dennison, and Howard envisioned the production of high-quality but inexpensive watches, made cheaply by having interchangeable parts. It took lots of money to reach the standard they wanted, using dials, jewels, and plates with high quality finishes. These in turn needed retooling and new investment, and they were running into problems.

Although their idea was to use interchangeable parts, and it was their goal to make money doing that, they hadn't reached the break-even turn, largely because they were still learning to do it. They made several styles of watches, each with its own set of problems and solutions and quality control.

The Waltham Watch Factory buildings still stand on Woerd Avenue.

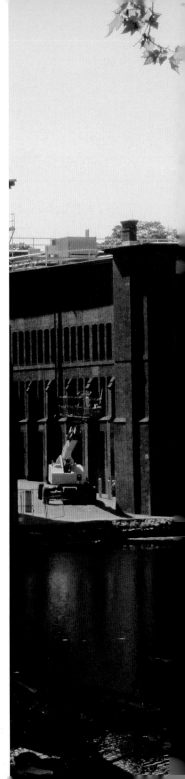

From Mt. Feake Cemetery across the river, you can appreciate the Queen Anne and Romanesque architectural features.

New ideas often need a break-in period. These can be discouraging when an inventor or manufacturer has high hopes and a bright idea, but they are part of the toil and trouble that have to be stirred into part of the brew of success, and they are often an important ingredient for staying the course. After an extended period they were able to adjust their watch making and make their products better than those of their competitors.

By that time they were ready to move. They wanted a better manufacturing environment and were building a new factory in Waltham that wouldn't have all the dust that got into the precision-tooled parts. The company was renamed "American Horology Company." The first watches made for the public were produced in 1853, and the name was changed to Boston Watch Company. The company moved to its new Waltham factory in 1854.

They built their factory (at the time the world's largest brick structure) on the banks of the Charles River and renamed it Waltham Watch. Over the century ahead, Waltham Watches became a known national brand. More than 40 million were produced, and they sold well. Waltham watches fit nicely into the niche of middle-class Americans who were on the rise during that interval in our history; they needed affordable watches that ran well.

It did well during the Civil War, and one reason might have been that President Lincoln wore one at Gettysburg, according to his biographer Carl Sandburg. The factory had stayed in operation during the war and stayed ahead of competitors by cutting expenses—a good strategy for anyone in financial trouble.

Their pioneering techniques of mass production and interchangeable parts were copied everywhere and helped to bring about our country's manufacturing success. A visit from Henry Ford inspired his later use of the assembly line to make his Model T and other cars. The "Waltham" was the only 100% American-made watch. Waltham became known as the "Watch City."

The company supplied railroad chronometers to American and foreign railroads and in 1876 revealed the first automatic screw making machine

At the Philadelphia Centennial Exposition, held that year, Waltham won the gold medal for watch precision.

Waltham continued to manufacture watches until 1957. It is still possible to purchase modern quartz watches that bear the Waltham name, but these watches are not related in any way to the "genuine" American Waltham Watch Company.

The Waltham works went on to produce other fine instruments like speedometers, compasses, and time fuses. Watchmaking in Waltham had long stopped when the plant closed in 1994. The works was and is located next to the east bank of the Charles River before it makes the major bend and heads toward Watertown. Both river and railroad were important modes of transportation in the mid-nineteenth century and one was a significant source of power. The building is undergoing renovation for other uses.

The heart of Waltham is Moody Street. In an earlier era, a fine department store, Grover Cronin, graced the street with its Art Deco façade and its quality goods. In mid-century, the store held parades at Easter and Christmas that drew as many as 200,000 viewers. But even before the store closed in 1989, the street had become seamy and depressed.

The city used federal block grants to bring new stores, restaurants, and a new Embassy Theatre to revitalize the area. The old Grover Cronin site was developed into Cronin's Landing, an apartment complex that preserved the Art Deco façade and ground floor retail. Across the Moody Street Bridge is the Riverwalk, under control of the state Department of Recreation and Conservation (DRC). The Waltham rail station is along this strip as well, while east across the bridge is Landry Park, which has views of the dam and waterfall, its fish ladder and the former Boston Manufacturing building, whose spaces have been changed into senior housing, artist's studios, and the Charles River Museum of Industry.

Up and down this river and others, mills were built, thrived, declined, and were abandoned. Some remained ruins or became blazing infernos at the hands of criminals. A few found other uses. Waltham appears to have set a fine example for what is possible.

As the Charles flows east, through Waltham, Newton, and Watertown, it has four dams, the last of them just above Watertown Square. Each had industrial uses. They lie about one mile apart from one another.

Rehabilitation, in phases, will include offices, retail and loft style residences.

Watches and textiles were not all that Waltham was. Around the turn of the twentieth century it made cars, too. Waltham was home to the Metz and the first production motorcycle in the U.S.

More than that, it was home to the Fernald State School, which in the limited understanding of its day, was a state-of-the-art institution for people with what we now call developmental disabilities. Fernald is the oldest institution for that purpose that was publicly funded.

But it began as a Victorian-style "sanatorium" and became a place for medical experiments in eugenics research, which became controversial and led to greater regulation.

Perhaps its original name will give a better idea. It was first called the Massachusetts School for Idiotic Children, formed by Samuel Gridley Howe with help from the state. The intent was good, but overcrowding and poor living conditions as well as abuse gave the school a bad name until improvements were made in the 1970s.

Waltham also has several large estates, notably Gore Place, built in 1806 for former governor Christopher Gore and the Robert Treat Paine Estate, designed for the nineteenth-century philanthropist by noted Boston architect Henry Hobson Richardson and landscape architect Frederick Law Olmsted. There is also the 400-acre Lyman Estate built for Boston merchant Theodore Lyman.

Cronin's Landing casts a reflection over the whole Moody Street renewal area.

The Charles slips below the bridge at Moody Street.

Fish ladders provide
piscine pass-through
at Moody Street.

The rapids below Moody Street Dam

Looking east from Moody,
the high-rise housing is on
Pine St. near Beaver Brook.

20.

Some $9 million in federal and state grants allowed the construction of a bicycle and walking path from Norumbega Park in Auburndale, along the Charles River to Moody Street in Waltham, then by way of a specially built walking and cycling bridge over the river to Watertown Square and then along existing paths to Boston's Museum of Science.

Granite pillars engraved with the image of a blue heron mark the six- to nine-foot-wide pathway, which varies from a soft, sandy-looking surface to sturdy boardwalks.

"It's probably the single most significant thing that's been done for the river since 1950," said Robert Zimmerman, executive director of the Charles River Watershed Association. Founded in 1965, the association promotes the cleaning up of the river and its surroundings. "I can't tell you how remarkable it is this is being done," Zimmerman said.

Until the environmental movement in the 1970s, few cared to go anywhere near the river because it was so filthy. Groups like the watershed association routinely fished cars, bicycles, tires, shopping carts, and barrels of "God knows what" out of the river, said Zimmerman. Now "the water quality is excellent," he said, despite a muddy brown appearance that's caused by natural tannins and the river's leisurely flow.

Perhaps the most dramatic piece of the new pathway is the Blue Heron Bridge, a 140-foot suspension bridge for pedestrians that crosses the river by Cheesecake Brook in Newton. Hidden by industrial and commercial buildings, including a Super Stop & Shop, the bridge serves as a graceful link between Newton and the Watertown/Waltham line. Traversing this tranquil trail, one is likely to

CHARLES RIVER RESERVATION

Blue Heron signs mark walkways administered by the
Massachusetts Department of Conservation and Recreation.

Blue Heron footbridge and walkways between Warertown and Newton is hidden
from most civilization.

Upper Charles walkway

The river has many secluded spots.

Walkway in Watertown

A quiet glen near the walkway

reflect on the impression that the various parts of the Charles, hidden as they are from one another by the canopy of trees and the gentle bends and curves, open upon small but satisfying vistas and that the improvements made by local organizations have afforded visitors recreational pleasures they may have been quite unaware of.

"Rivers like the Charles weren't treated well," said Zimmerman. "For many years, people didn't look at the recreational value, they looked at it as a way to take waste away."

Indeed, the plan's biggest hurdle early on was the large number of illegal encroachments by businesses and homeowners on public land, such as parking lots, chain-link fences, patios, and rusting equipment on the riverbanks. A 1992 land survey identified more than 90 encroachments in the way of the proposed path.

In many cases, the intrusions had gone on for so long "many landowners were surprised to learn they didn't own the land," said Daniel Driscoll, a senior state planner whose early days on

the project were spent negotiating with abutters.

Since then, the state has been able to reclaim property through scenic easements and land gifts from a number of formerly encroaching businesses. Some, like Sasaki Associates in Watertown, have even agreed to pay for maintenance of overlook decks and boardwalks next to their buildings.

The Upper Charles River Reservation continues with walkways as far south as West Roxbury. Native plant life has also been restored along the river, and this has brought back local birds and wildlife.

The view south from Riverwalk, Waltham

Settlers like John Jackson and later John Woodward and John Staples came to the northern part of Newton, but still another John established Clark's Mill, a sawmill at the Upper Falls. It was he who brought industry to the town.

The population of Newton Upper Falls amounted to only a few families, but it was one of the most dynamic parts of early Newton. Upper Falls was one of the first six villages, and it kept its fitting name even when the town was incorporated. Remarkably, the village has in many ways remained as it was. It is now a historical district with more than 150 structures, many of them happily undisturbed.

At the very time the town of Newton was incorporated in 1688, John Clark was building his sawmill, the first industry of any type on the Charles River in Newton. A gristmill followed in 1710, and five years later a fulling mill to pound and shrink woolen cloth. In later years, but in the same century, this collection of buildings was joined by others—four that made snuff, a wire mill, a screw factory, a blacksmith shop, and one used for annealing or hardening iron and steel.

In 1723, Boston's Thomas Handasyd Perkins built a large cotton mill on the site, calling it Eliot Manufacturing Company for his father-in-law. Before the Perkins' enterprise began their operations, most of the old Eliot snuff mills and other industrial buildings were removed.

The Upper Falls, located close to Needham on the Charles, in the southern part of Newton, begin a rapid drop after a fairly long, gradual flow. This sharp descent was caused 10,000 years earlier by a glacier whose movement was delayed when it reached the rocky area at the Upper Falls.

As the glacier reached the ledge of Roxbury Pudding Stone (made up of lava and loose stone) on Prospect Hill, it towered at nearly a mile in height. But as its melting snow and ice and mixed boulders slid down the rock, they crashed into the rocky mass below, boring a hole in the ledge with a granite boulder serving as its drill as it rotated during the deluge.

The hole it made was partly torn away, leaving a smooth partial hole that may still be seen today near Eliot Street as the Upper Falls Pothole.

The glacial material made a path in the softer rock and reached lower ground leaving a pathway to the sea. The area of rapid descent is known as Hemlock Gorge, which became the route of the Charles River. At that point it drops 26 feet in a few hundred feet, and from there the river finds its largely meandering path toward Boston Harbor.

The glacier had not only left a path for the river, it had created the means for John Clark to harness the power of the falling water to turn the wheel of his mill and establish Newton Upper Falls.

A grant of weir lands was given to Thomas Mayhew of Watertown. They were on the south side of the Charles, and he also had 500 acres of land farther south, and land where the village of Upper Falls would stand.

About half of the property once owned by Mayhew was bought in 1658 by John Kenrick in the section east of the village where Kenrick's Bridge crosses from Newton into Needham near Cutter Lake, Kenrick Street, and the industrial park along Route 128 (U.S. 95). Kenrick's name was linked with another famous family when his great, great granddaughter, Anna Kenrick married a revolutionary general, Benjamin Pierce, and had a son, Franklin Pierce, who became 14th President of the U.S. (He was a friend of Longfellow as well.)

A weir was used by the Algonquins on the downriver side of the upper falls.

The river is said to have originally been named *Quinobequin* "the river that circles around," by the Pumkapoag tribe of the Algonquin Indians, and it does do just that. A good example is the stretch between Upper and Lower Falls, a short distance as the crow flies, but a roundabout journey for the river.

Those same Native Americans with their weir, caught both freshwater and saltwater fish since the falls and rapids by Clark's Mill were the turnaround point for fish from the ocean. The

Algonquins had a unique way of catching fish like salmon, shad, and alewives at their upriver weir and also near the Watertown dam. Above the dam fresh water fish were caught as they headed downstream.

The men of the tribe "swept" the fish downstream into the weir. They made "brooms" by cutting saplings, and then stripping off the lower branches from the young trees. The tops were then used like water brooms, one brave dipping one of these implements deeply into the water as another brave paddled the canoe. This phalanx of sweepers drove many of the fish ahead of them to where the women of the tribe were waiting at the weir in shallow water with a net of woven reeds. The caught fish were dragged ashore, cleaned, and smoked above open fires, then stored for the winter in caves.

These fishing rights were so ancient and so important that the tribes would not sell their lands without retaining their rights to fish in these rivers for perpetuity.

A story has it that some early settlers heading upriver from Watertown came to Hemlock Gorge in 1636, but were so scared by the noisy, rushing waters and the darkness of the hemlock-shaded area as well as by the Native Americans in the shadows on the banks that they decided to keep going, and did so until they reached the sunny open plains where Dedham is now.

A town park was created in 1893 along the river at Hemlock Gorge. It had a dance pavilion, an orchestra, and refreshment stand with rows of seats in a natural amphitheater, as well as amusements for children. On Sunday afternoon, large crowds came and at night the grounds were illuminated.

Cook's Bridge over the Charles River at Eliot Street still relies on the original arches of the "cartbridge" built about 1714. It is believed to be the same bridge that spanned the river nearly 300 years ago. I drove over it in the spring of 2011, and didn't give it a thought. I should have, if only for its history. The short span is named for Captain Robert Cook who bought forty acres of land at that spot from the Native Americans at the turn of the eighteenth century. The short bridge was widened one hundred

Cook's Bridge at Upper Falls and Needham

years later. They used the original stone "facing," while the sidewalk was extended out from the bridge on the north side.

What's surprising about Newton Upper Falls and its interaction with the Charles River is not that the area's original and later settlers took advantage of its natural resources, but that the natural features may still be seen, understood, and appreciated and that many of the old buildings like the Silk Mill are still there for those who want to envision their colonial past and think about the trail from then to now. Such is history if we care to consider it. Upper Falls will let you do that, and it's an easy visit just off major highways, with a park at the Hemlock Gorge site.

Rapids at silk mill, Upper Falls

Ducks at Hemlock Bridge

Quinobequin Road between Upper and Lower Falls

Quinobequin Road winds between the upper and lower falls, the next set of rapids and short falls. Newton Lower Falls is a brief stretch of the river way between Wellesley to the west and Newton just east of that. It's an area that today is part of the Washington Street-Route 16 descent toward the present Route 128 before the land and the road turn upwards toward the Newton-Wellesley Hospital—all names known well to those who follow the Boston Marathon, which begins at the source of the Charles in Hopkinton.

The Charles flows flatly along Quinobequin Road.

Early Newton history goes back to the Upper Falls, as we have seen, and also the Lower Falls, two miles farther downstream. This small area also features rapids and waterfalls that were once harnessed to waterwheels and mills to provide power for the early settlements along the Charles. Newton Lower Falls had dams at each of three places where the water dropped, a sixteen-foot drop being the largest. The Charles and these falls are still quietly evident along Washington Street and the streets springing from it.

The earliest of these mills goes back to 1704 and brings us the names of John Hubbard and Caleb Church, who had the Yankee ingenuity to build a dam at the appropriate location on the Newton side of the Lower Falls. Unlike the earlier mills at Upper Falls, this dam was fashioned to power an ironworks.

And why an ironworks? you may wonder. That was because Newton was an agricultural area and it needed things like tools and farm implements. It needed lots of them and soon—a local manufactory for such iron items made good sense.

Lower Falls made sense, too. It was a good place to produce products in local demand and so dams were built and mills developed and a road was set out—today's Washington Street-Route 16—which dipped down to the river and up the hill beyond and brought houses for workers and mill-owners alike. By the time the 1700s came to an end, ten families were living along this stretch, all of them associated with activities at the dams at Lower Falls.

History hints to us that once a population has found a power source and has established industry at a particular place, it tends to continue that trend.

That's what happened at Lower Falls. As years went by, and the seventeenth century gave way to the industrial-minded eighteenth and nineteenth, manufacturing continued at these same locales, albeit small in scale. This was no Pittsburgh. In fact, it remained unintentionally quaint, a nice quality today.

By the year 1816, six paper mills had clustered in the Lower Mills locale and the population at the river-crossing stabilized as Lower Mills became a thriving industrial village with 405 people and 33 houses by the year 1823.

That village, small though it was, became a regular stop on the stagecoach route with three trips into Boston a week. As befits such transportation hubs then and now, it had taverns, shops, and of course in those days, a church. It had, additionally, Newton's first fire company to protect all those buildings and people.

But as the nineteenth century tickered off its final years, such small-time developments as Lower Falls fell by the wayside as industry flourished elsewhere in Massachusetts and up the coast to Maine where papermaking centers grew on a larger scale, rendering Lower Mills industries an afterthought.

Then, when Route 128 was built parallel to the Charles in the early 1950s, and urban renewal became fashionable two decades later, the quaint village-like ambiance of this hamlet on the Charles was allowed to disintegrate. Historic landmarks vanished, along with the homes of laborers, older churches, and schools, all of which held no purchase on the loyalty of inhabitants of that era when history was oft consigned to the rubbish bin in the name of "progress."

In the end, only remnants survived from the once prosperous village of mills and their workers, especially along Washington Street, but the river was more placid.

Those who would hunt for links with the historic past must explore the side streets of the village. Even the historic Pillar House Restaurant has disappeared from Quinobequin Road where it long stood as a memento of earlier times within view of travelers on the Yankee Highway. It has since been closed, taken apart and moved in large part to Lincoln where a private party has reconstructed many of its historic parts.

The erstwhile restaurant was once the home of Solomon Curtis, one of the Lower Falls papermakers who owned Jackson Mill and also the Eliot Mills at Upper Falls during the 1700s.

Cords of water at Newton Lower Falls

Here is the Lower Falls ladder—for fish.

Ducks discover quiet water between Cordingly Falls and Lower Falls.

Boating upstream at Concord Street, Newton/Weston

Those who have enjoyed fine dining and a nostalgic environment at the Pillar House might like to know that someone who lived in this Greek Revival style building in 1845 made the fine paper used for the very best books in those days, when books were owned mostly by the rich. They are more likely to know that the house that looked like a Greek Temple and had small but elegant rooms, served other wealthy people as a restaurant for the last half of the twentieth century, closing in 2001—a Wellesley odyssey.

The Charles behind Walnut Street, Newton/Wellesley

Trees and their reflections frame a quiet spot above Newton Lower Falls.

The aqueducts of Newton

23

If you look at a map of Newton or, better still, an aerial view of the Charles River area at the Upper and Lower Falls, you may notice that the two aqueducts, which run through the town, form two sides of an open triangle as they enter Newton from the west across the Charles River near the Lower Falls and at Upper Falls. As they cross the river they are about a mile apart, but they converge in a vertex of two rays at Four Corners near the Newton Centre Playground.

If there were a base for this triangle, it would line up roughly with Quinobequin Road, which runs along the river between Route 9 near the Upper Falls to Route 16 at Lower Falls.

The aqueducts make a curious feature on the landscape, looking for all the world like green ribbons as seen from the air. More significantly, the tops of them offer walking paths for athletes, adults, and school groups who have followed them over the years as they cut through more circuitous routes and provide safe and fascinating paths of transportation.

Most of the trails along the aqueducts offer tranquil thrusts into natural areas with birds that can immerse you among wildlife, trees, flowers, vines, and other flora—here are quiet glades not far from the bustle of civilization, green surroundings that residents may readily use.

Since they cross streets and intersections at grade level, the aqueducts provide many access points for shorter and longer walks and hikes, jaunts by joggers, and easy routes for cyclists in Newton and in towns beyond, like Wellesley and Needham.

Many Newton residents will know them well; others will not. They are sure to provide an intriguing mystery for non-residents who could also use the trails for exercise as well as the pursuit of the extraordinary.

There are two of these aqueducts, as mentioned, and they were once used to transport water to Boston from reservoirs in the Sudbury River and Lake Cochituate. When the transported water quality began to deteriorate, they were abandoned, and came under the control of Newton and of the Metropolitan District Commission.

Echo Bridge, near Route 9, part of the aqueduct system from Sudbury River.

The aqueducts are another good example of creative reuse in conjunction with conservation and recreation. Built to carry water to the core city, much as Roman aqueducts did in centuries gone by, they now refresh in other ways and they do so without great expense and without having to tear up suburban tracts and displace people as a major highway would have done.

There's also a lesson for planners and conservationists in the history of these structures, just as there was, in a more destructive way, a lesson in the urban renewal that took place at the same time—the 1950s and 1960s. At that time, pieces of the Cochituate Aqueduct were sold to private homeowners. That had the same effect as selling pieces of beachfront or waterfront to individuals. It blocked public access and it's doubtful whether that can be corrected, at least not without major expenditures of public funds, now unavailable.

Their current use also puts them in play so that other, adverse uses are blocked. If community use is well-established over an extended period, it will be difficult to impose other, inappropriate uses.

24

A scarcity of land after the Great Migration of Puritans brought settlers to Dedham in 1635, when the General Court of Massachusetts Bay Colony permitted the establishment of Concord and Dedham as two inland towns.

Since early settlers engaged in farming and grazing, they needed more land, and that usually meant outlying towns had to be founded. Also, it was believed that attacks from Native Americans in the interior were likely, so inland towns would provide outposts.

Most of the settlers in Dedham came from Watertown and Roxbury. The leaders among them were middle-class people from around the town of Dedham in England, so the General Court gave the town that name. It was a huge area, however, and included such Charles River towns as Needham, Wellesley, Dover, Norwood, Walpole, Westwood, Wrentham, Medfield, Medway, Mendon, Millis, Norfolk, and Bellingham. It also included Sherborn and Natick, Foxborough and Franklin.

When King Philip's War did come in 1675–76, the town of Dedham was protected by rivers and marshes and a treeless plain, so it was not attacked, though Medfield and Wrentham were. One early colonist, Jonathan Fairbanks, built a house for himself, which is today the oldest house in North America.

In a typical Puritan way, Dedham instituted a policy of keeping out or removing people who were troublesome or who couldn't make their own livings.

Dedham had a singular pre-Revolution event—the holding of a Suffolk County Convention at Woodward Tavern at about the location of today's Norfolk County Court (Dedham later became the shire town of Norfolk County). Dedham adopted the Suffolk Resolves, and later, Paul Revere would introduce them to Philadelphia, which would do the same.

Becoming the shire town in 1793 brought lawyers, politicians, and visitors on county business to Dedham and led to it shedding its Puritan insularity and becoming a transportation center. The Norfolk and Bristol Turnpike was built through Dedham in 1803, becoming the main route between Boston and Providence, and a year later the Hartford and Dedham Turnpike (now Route 109) led westward to eastern Connecticut. Dedham added inns and taverns and became a way station on the mail route or Post Road between Boston and New York, which was also the route used by stagecoaches and later by the railroad.

The Boston and Providence Railroad built a branch from Readville (then in Dedham) to its main line, the Norfolk County Railroad was built in 1848 from Dedham to Walpole, and in 1854 the Boston and New York Central ran through the town. Industries made good use of the advances of transportation, which allowed them to develop.

The potential for this began much earlier, when, in 1637, Mother Brook was dug as a canal between the Charles and Neponset Rivers via East Brook. The part of this waterway that was man-made rather than natural is considered the first canal in America made by English settlers. Though both the Charles and Neponset were rather flat at this point, there was a 40-foot difference in their elevation and this provided Dedham with its only source of waterpower until well into the twentieth century.

This canal diverted water from the Charles, and Newton later protested to the General Court. Judge Abraham Fuller presented the Newton case, and he seldom lost. It was said that his voice was so powerful that when he called his cows it could be heard a mile away. His voice was heard in this case, which was settled in 1831 and Dedham was allowed to divert only a third of the water flow from the Charles thereafter.

Mother Brook was dug to support a corn mill, and the town offered sixty acres of land to whomever would build one. John Elderkin built one in 1641 in East Dedham and evidently built it well, for it lasted 250 years. Today it can play its diversionary role at a time of flood when it can serve as a spillway to shunt a greater quantity of water than usual out of the watershed.

In later years mills were built to roll copper for coins, for a brush factory, a wire factory, three different paper mills, and an early loom. By 1845 these mills provided those products plus thread, chairs, boots, cigars, and tools, and they made Dedham an economic powerhouse.

Dedham voted to begin the first taxpayer funded public school in 1644. Rev. Ralph Wheelock became its teacher—presumably the first public school teacher in Massachusetts. However, three years later the General Court decided that every town of 50 or more families must have a public school, so Massachusetts was a leader in that area, and Dedham led Massachusetts.

Late in the decade, with Dedham becoming crowded, Rev. Wheelock was named to head a new township farther upriver called Medfield where he also taught school.

Dedham Common on the former Dedham-Hartford Turnpike (now Rte.109)

Rivermoor Park, West Roxbury

The towns along the Charles River Basin had reasonable access to Boston, via the river or land routes. That was also true of Watertown, Waltham, and parts of Newton and even Dedham. Those towns on the west side were isolated to some extent, at least until the railroads were built, so they developed later and more slowly. They remain more suburban than most towns on the east, north, or south sides of the river. Bridges and roads came in the early eighteenth century

Weston

This town on the west bank was located on the Boston Post Road, and though largely agricultural, it had inns and taverns that brought travelers—The Golden Ball and Josiah Smith taverns still exist. Once part of Watertown, those who remained behind called it "the west pine meadow" or "the farms." A gristmill was built on Stony Brook near the Charles in 1679 and later a cotton mill.

It became a separate town in 1713. The post road (now Route 20) diminished in importance after the Boston and Worcester road (now Route 9) was built.

Unlike other towns, Weston had little Native American activity, even along the river. It may have acted as a buffer between various tribes. The population remained low until after 1875. Immigrant groups settled during that period, and some wealthy people from Boston built country estates in the town.

The town is on a rugged upland with little viable agricultural land or waterpower. Weston had some shoemaking, factories that made textile machinery, an organ company, and some small mills. In the late nineteenth century, the Hastings Hook Organ Company was built there, but it caught fire in the early 1900s. The fire department responded, running their hoses into a pond on the other side of a railroad track. However, a train went by, cut the hoses and doomed the firefighting effort. The organs piped no more.

Industry never really took hold, nor did farming, but those country estates seemed a good idea to Bostonians, and that became the trend.

Weston today is known as a wealthy suburb of Boston with a fine school system.

Kayaker cruising near Martin Golf Course

Weston: Historic First Parish Church

Feathers among the ripples, Weston

Wellesley Town Hall

Wellesley

Its early history was as Needham's west precinct, and the western part of town (where Wellesley College is now) was part of Natick. In fact, Rev. John Eliot of South Natick and the Praying Towns was their chief engineer and helped them build a sawmill on Waban Brook. Wellesley Hills also had a Native American connection. It was bought from a gentleman named Magus, a Christian Native American who had fought against King Phillip. A handful of settlers came to the area around the Charles River where the town of Wellesley is now located, and liked it well enough to call the town "Contentment." Many residents might still describe their situation in town using that word, or they might speak of pride.

In fact, in the year 1981, a weeklong Centennial Celebration gave newcomers a chance to learn more about their town, its history, and its many fine qualities. Of course the early settlers came more than 100 years before that. John Hubbard had built a forge and iron mill at Lower Falls in 1703, but papermaking became the main industry of that area.

Originally part of the Dedham grant and then part of Needham, Wellesley had few settlers until after King Philip's War and especially into the 1700s. Many of the settlers came from Newton or Watertown, but some also came from the west—Natick, Sherborn, Sudbury, or from Dedham and Needham to the south. The main line of settlement was along today's Washington Street from the Lower Falls. Some of that was at today's Wellesley Square and at Wellesley Hills near the Worcester road.

The early days of the town had seen agriculture and lumbering as well as some milling along the lower falls. Transportation had improved with two railroad stations built in the 1880s, a trolley line along Washington Street in the 1890s and another from Boston and Brookline along Route 9 in the early 1900s. The population grew apace in that era, including a large number of foreign-born.

Henry Durant came to Wellesley and in 1875 founded a college for women, Wellesley College, across from Lake Waban on the road to Natick. He named it for his next-door neighbor Horatio Hollis Hunnewell, whose mansion had been named "Wellesley" in commemoration of his wife who was a Welles. Durant and Hunnewell, along with Joseph Fiske, organized residents to work for separation from Needham, and Wellesley would be the name of the town, too. A town meeting was held at town hall, which served as the poor farm and which, ironically, would later become the Wellesley Country Club. In 1881, the state legislature named the new town Wellesley. Since then, town leadership has demanded the best for their town. With money, political know-how, and a motivated populace, they have been successful. It was the first town in America to adopt zoning laws and it is a beautiful, well-planned town.

Needham

The town of Needham began on the Great Plain, the long flatland on the south side of the Charles across from Newton and Dedham. The plain had been bought from Chief Nahaton in 1680, with the sachem keeping forty acres of it near Upper Falls where his tribe had a fish weir. Needham used the plain to grow grain, but even that was hard in the poor soil where the grains the Puritans had grown in England grew poorly if at all.

The plains had belonged to Dedham, but Needham was founded there in 1711, adopting its name from the English town. The first industry was a paper mill at Charles River Village, built in 1796. The area thrived during the Civil War when one mill made "shoddy," a cloth fashioned of bits of used cloth mixed with new cloth, often used to make clothing for short-term use. It also had a mill that made manila paper.

Just before the Civil War (1853), the Charles River Railroad opened to Needham. It brought gravel from East Needham near the Charles to Back Bay from 1858 into the 1870s, leveling cliffs and ledges over that period.

Another industry that was unique to Needham along the Charles was knitting mills. Knitters had come there from the Midlands section of England and set up the same kinds of business south of the Charles. The most famous company was the William Carter Company, founded by a man of the same name in 1865 to make knitwear and children's clothing. Since 1990, its Needham Heights location has been occupied by an assisted living facility called Avery Manor. Some of its residents once worked at the factory, a Needham landmark for many years.

In the 1950s, Route 128 was built through Needham and brought high technology firms during the post World War II boom (as it did to Waltham and other towns along the Charles). As the Charles constitutes an arc around Boston, in this middle area the highway runs mostly parallel to the river. The Charles passes under Route 128 three times, once each in Dedham, Newton. and Weston.

The corner of Highland, Great Plain, and Dedham Avenues, Needham

The Charles cuts through Cutter Park, Needham

113

The Charles River has its source in Hopkinton and winds its way south from there to near the Rhode Island border before heading northeast to Wellesley and then east to Dedham where it takes a dip south again before heading north to Waltham and then on to Boston. Some 35 towns have at least a tributary contributing to the watershed, but the widest part of the river flows north from Dedham to the mouth.

The upstream area from Hopkinton south to Westwood consists mostly of small or mid-sized towns, each with its own history and some interesting features, though the river itself in these parts is mostly placid and seldom wide. Along with the streams, ponds, and aquifers that make up this part of the watershed, the area plays the part of a natural storage area, and contributes to flood-control, although population buildup threatens this function as well.

This is all part of the Charles River Natural Storage Area, an inner kingdom of more than 8,000 acres in the middle and upper watershed of the river that has become protected land. From a field office at West Hill Dam, the U.S. Army Corps of Engineers and Massachusetts Division of Fisheries and Wildlife administer scattered wetlands that provide flood control and water storage, among other things. Much of the area is forested, but it also contains wetlands, lakes, and ponds.

The congressional act that created this area provided for its permanent protection, including flood control and use of the area for recreation and open space. All land that has been acquired has to be preserved in its natural state, and changes in natural drainage are not allowed. This also acts as a brake on development of course. And it provides an opportunity for hiking, canoeing, fishing, bird watching, and cross-country skiing as well as walking.

The Charles River Watershed Association (CRWA) focused on flood control in the 1980s and continues working to improve the ecology of the area. Its early work helped to preserve 8,000 acres of wetlands, which in turn alleviated downstream flooding, preserved natural habitats for wildlife, and replenished and purified water for other uses.

As a result of their work, the number of fish have been replenished and about three-quarters of the river is suitable for swimming. However, the encroachment of development due to I-495 continues to pose problems as do pollution, expanded sewer systems, and demands for drinking water.

Still, conditions are far better than in the 1960s when wastewater treatment plants overflowed and factories added toxic materials that killed fish and made the river turn orange, along with the abandoned cars, leaching from town dumps, and strange odors. The CRWA has also helped to clean up the watershed and to promote modern wastewater plants on the upper Charles.

The Charles River Restoration Project began in 1992. It found that land along its territory had been encroached upon in 92 places. Once they had reclaimed these, it was able to construct a greenway along the river as far down as Watertown Sq. through Newton, Waltham, and Weston to the Lakes District. Much of the watershed district now has walking paths, and there are also bicycle paths.

Map of the Charles River Watershed system, *courtesy of Charles River Watershed Association*

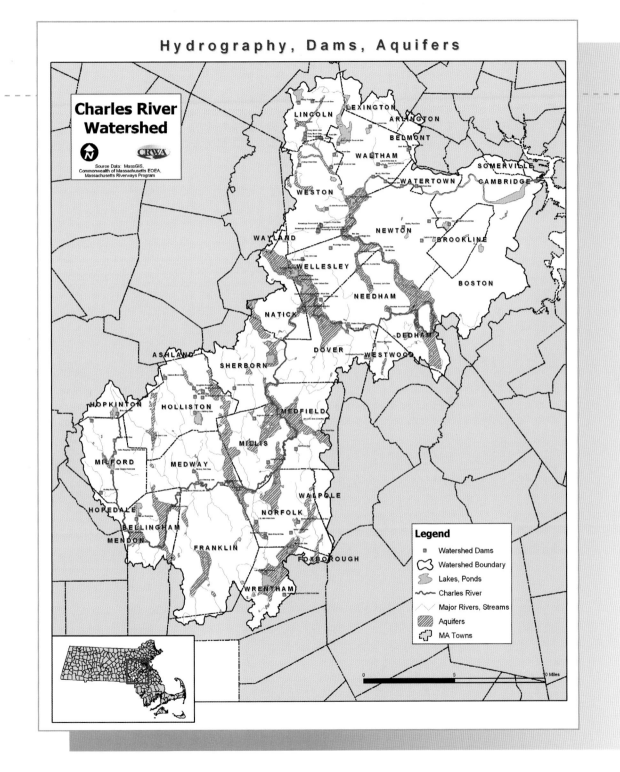

Hydrography, Dams, Aquifers

Charles River Watershed

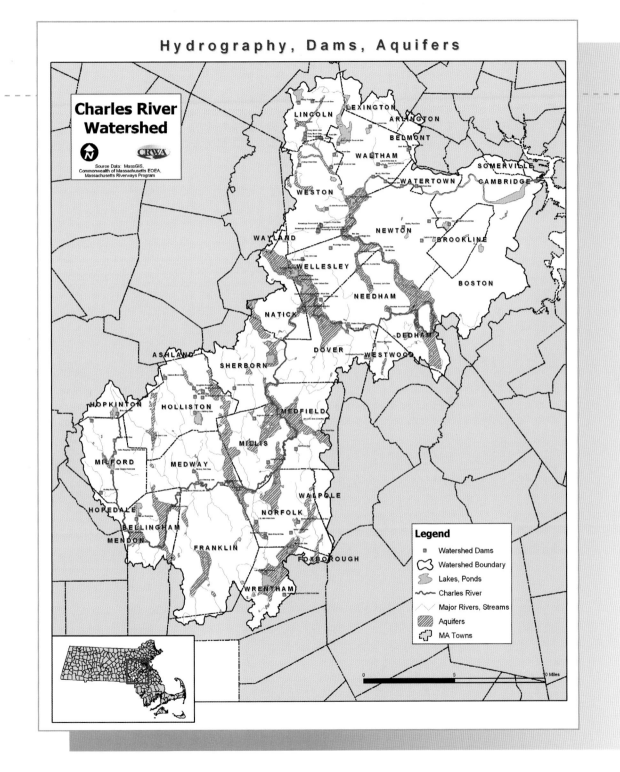

Source Data: MassGIS,
Commonwealth of Massachusetts EOEA,
Massachusetts Riverways Program

CRWA

LINCOLN
LEXINGTON
ARLINGTON
BELMONT
WALTHAM
SOMERVILLE
WATERTOWN
CAMBRIDGE
WESTON
NEWTON
BROOKLINE
WAYLAND
WELLESLEY
BOSTON
NEEDHAM
NATICK
DEDHAM
DOVER
WESTWOOD
ASHLAND
SHERBORN
HOPKINTON
HOLLISTON
MEDFIELD
MILLIS
MILFORD
MEDWAY
HOPEDALE
NORFOLK
WALPOLE
BELLINGHAM
MENDON
FRANKLIN
FOXBOROUGH
WRENTHAM

Legend

- Watershed Dams
- Watershed Boundary
- Lakes, Ponds
- Charles River
- Major Rivers, Streams
- Aquifers
- MA Towns

0   5   10 Miles

Hopkinton

Echo Lake in Hopkinton is the approximate source of the Charles, which traces from there a low gradient with extensive wetlands. Nearby is also the source of the Blackstone River, which flows south through Worcester County into Rhode Island.

The center of Hopkinton once had nine plants that made boots and shoes and straw bonnets, too, but industry took no major hold on the town, and its slow growth preserved a nineteenth-century look.

The town had a mystic pull as well because the waters that flowed from a large swamp south of Pond Street into Lake Whitehall were thought to have magical healing powers, which attracted tourists. The area became a mini-resort, and stagecoaches brought visitors to the Hopkinton Hotel to try the mineral baths. They were the hottest attraction until the Boston Marathon established its starting point there in 1897. That annual event brought a new tonic to the town.

However, as of 2011, when two runners bested the world record, we have learned that the course of the Marathon—like that of the Charles River—has a decided fall off in elevation and cannot qualify athletes for the official records.

The town has another Hopkinton to Boston story, too. Sir Henry Frankland, collector of taxes in Boston for the crown in colonial days, met a poor fisherman's daughter, Agnes Surriage, in a Marblehead tavern where she was scrubbing floors. He paid for her education, and she then moved in with him, which was unacceptable to Boston aristocracy, so he built a mansion in Hopkinton for them instead.

Sited on 500 hilly and wooded acres with views of New Hampshire, the home had chimneys of Italian marble, houses for servants, greenhouses, and grounds with rare trees and imported plants.

Frankland and his wealthy invited guests spent mornings fox hunting, afternoons listening to chamber music, and evenings with continental banquets. Late at night and into the wee hours, Frankland and his friends had drinking bouts in which he used a glass with a false bottom to drink the others under his ample table. Unlike in Boston, here in Hopkinton, Frankland lived as he liked.

Later, when he and Agnes were married in Portugal, he bought a house on the other end of the river in Boston. He now held parties in both places, riding his pony up and down the wide staircases of his opulent Boston place, but when Henry died, Agnes returned to Hopkinton until the Revolution when she left the country.

Holliston

This town has feeder streams to the Charles, which runs just south of its border, and the Upper Charles River Trail runs through the town. That's one of those recreational trails.

One point of interest is Balancing Rock, on the side of Route 16. The boulder is about twenty-by-ten-by-six feet in size and weights more than five tons. It appears to be balanced on a granite ledge, looking quite easy to dislodge. But not so. In November of 1789, General George Washington was traveling from New York to Boston when his route took him through Holliston. Washington made an entry in his diary about the road that would one day bear his name:

> …an indifferent road, diversified by good and bad land, cultivated and in woods, some high barren, others low, wet and piney.

He might have mentioned his encounter with the rock. We can only say that legend has it that George saw its balancing act as a challenge and went at it with a will, joining others of his party in trying to move it, without noticeable effect. Others have tried over the years, but it remains as it was, standing today on what has become the grounds of a community of older adults.

Balancing Boulder

Milford

The Charles River runs the length of town from north to south including the town center. It drops 125 feet and in the early days it provided power for two mill sites, one at the center, the other at Wildcat Pond. Boot and shoe making factories were also established along the Mill River. When the Boston & Albany RR came through town in the middle 1800s, these factories were expanded and many Irish immigrants came to work in them.

A town of 25,000, Milford also developed a major granite industry and became known for its pink granite, used for public buildings and memorials around the country and beyond, including both the old and new sections of the Boston Public Library.

Hopedale

Hopedale has a unique history in that it was formed as a Utopian town in 1842 by Adam Ballou and the Practical Christians. Ballou's hope was to "feed, clothe, educate and maintain our families better than is now done by the middling class of society."

In its early days, the members of this religious community lived like a family under a single roof with the goal of doing so in harmony and peace. Its members also supported peace movements, the abolition of capital punishment, and especially the abolition of slavery.

Eventually non-members outnumbered members in the town and things began to change. It became home to the Draper Corporation, the largest maker of textile looms in the U.S.

Mendon

This town has a history surprisingly different from those around it.

Mendon was first settled in 1660, by families from Weymouth and Braintree, but was the location of the first violence of King Philip's War—the mill was burned, along with most of the town, and several residents were killed.

Years later, Mendon became known as the town that did not let George Washington sleep there. An innkeeper's wife turned him away in 1789. Also, despite all the industrial towns around it that made boots or cotton products or machinery, Mendon is better known as an agricultural community. It became the town's role to feed the other towns.

Bellingham

This town lies south of the Charles and is also in the Blackstone River Valley, but it was slow to be settled and leisurely in its growth. It apparently (no one is sure) was named for a former governor of the Massachusetts Bay Colony.

Bellingham's appeal was diminished by its marshy and rocky land with many trees. It wasn't much good for farming and it was hard to reach by road. Those travelers who passed that way usually passed through. It had no real growth spurt until Route 495 was built and lots of big box retailers with brand names moved in. Marshy soil didn't matter to them.

Perhaps the best-known citizen was one who was trying to fly below the radar and got caught. Deborah Sampson enlisted in the army at Bellingham during the Revolution disguised as a man. She was America's first woman soldier.

Medway

The valley of the Charles, from the falls in this town north to South Natick, kept its Native America name, *Boggestow*, which is now the name (with altered spelling) of a brook and pond.

It was along the Charles that mills were built, beginning in the early 1700s; 100 years later the mills produced cotton. The Medway Village Historic District is also located along the banks of the river in this watershed town. It was the first part of Medway to begin to grow; fortunately, it has more than 200 historic buildings remaining on its sixty acres where textile mills once stood, sustaining the small town with industry during the nineteenth century.

Here the Charles descended in falls in an area known by 1830 as Factory Village. Medway Village came into its own just as the Charles River experienced industrial expansion. This came in an unusual form inasmuch as the industrialization was broad rather than deep and included a variety of manufactories, not just one.

Medway Village expanded by attracting other businesses and bringing together a diverse community of people from various ethnic groups, an expansion that was only enhanced by the railroad when it rolled into Medway in the 1860s, bringing other factories.

Franklin

Due south of Medway and across the Charles lies Franklin, the first town in America named for Benjamin Franklin. Like today's towns that might name a bridge for someone or a stadium for a company, the new town hoped for a reciprocal gesture —they thought Ben Franklin might come through with some kind of ringing endorsement—like a bell.

Franklin might have lived where the Liberty Bell served as an icon, but he had also started the country's first lending library and he went that way instead. The former Bostonian showed his appreciation by sending the town a library of 116 religious volumes from London that became the starting point for America's First Public Library.

The potential of waterpower set the compass for the town's future. Its early farming and grazing soon took back seats to industry as the town's rivers brought cotton mills, factories that produced felt for hats, boots, and shoes, and mostly the surprisingly successful manufacture of straw bonnets.

Franklin is one of these towns with charmingly peculiar historical mementoes. For example, it is still home to the country's oldest one-room schoolhouse— the Red Brick School (National Register), which operated until 2008. The town is also the birthplace of Horace Mann, father of American education.

Millis

Railroad executive Lansing Millis, was the first to chair the selectmen in the town named for him, which was once a popular vacation spot with its location on the Charles. Even today, townsfolk canoe and kayak and take part in the annual cleanup.

Lansing made the town a rail center, which helped to bring economic growth, as did the Hartford and Dedham Turnpike (today's state road 109).

Transportation was significant in industrial growth as well. Millis has had some major companies that have created employment in the area. Waterpower allowed the establishment of Hinsdell's mill in the early days, and a steady growth in industries followed.

These included a bell foundry, manufacturers of organs and organ pipes, the Cliquot Club, and the Herman Shoe Company. Herman Shoe got its biggest boosts from boots, providing footwear for our military during the Spanish-American War and later in World War II. Next door to it stood the Clicquot Club, established by Henry Millis, son of Lancing.

Millis ginger played a role in the beverages that made Clicquot Club famous. It was used in making the first ginger ale in the U.S. The company went on to produce other beverages as well, and was the first to sell its sodas in cans. The company had more than a hundred factories and sold beverages around the world until it was bought out by Cott which went on to become part of Canada Dry.

The area near Causeway Street was once the center of industry in the town. Clay was dug from the ground and used to make bricks that were used to build homes and buildings southwest of Boston. Sand from the area was used to fill a runway at Logan Airport.

Another notable site is Great Black Swamp which separates Millis from Medfield and whose impassibility led to the forming of two distinct towns.

Some large estates were built near the sand pits. One of them belonged to Christian Herter, former Governor of Massachusetts and Secretary of State for the United States. His name is also attached to the other end of the Charles—a recreation area in Brighton, along the Charles, is named for him.

When George Washington traveled this way en route to Cambridge to take command of American forces, he stopped along the way, including at Richardson's Tavern in Millis which dates to 1720.

The town is known, too, for its "Millis Lights," an area so brilliant with Christmas decorations that it draws 7,000 cars a day during the Christmas season.

Norfolk

Settlers first came to Norfolk in 1669 in an attempt to populate the upper valley of the Charles, which was then the frontier. Even though the land was good for farming, settlers were reluctant to go there because it was so remote. When King Philip's War brought a raid on nearby Medfield, even those few farms were abandoned for a period. It later had some farms, grazing of livestock, orchards, and lumbering.

After the War of 1812 brought home the need for American industry, Norfolk established three cotton mills at Stony Brook. Later in that century, Campbell's paper mill opened at Highland Lake. It made heavy paper for wrapping and building.

The population saw an increase after 1925 when a hospital and state prison were built near the Walpole line, and it became more residential in the Pondville area during the 1940s.

One of the attractions of Norfolk is the Stony Brook Wildlife Sanctuary managed by Mass Audubon and Mass DCR. This is a 245-acre area of wetlands and wildlife preservation with a long boardwalk system that allows visitors to walk along the sides of Teal Marsh and Kingfisher Pond to view birds and butterflies in their habitat.

Medfield

As with many towns in the watershed region, Medfield was spun off from another town, in this case Dedham. Men from that town had begun to farm and graze their animals on the broad meadows and continuous plain that lie southwest of them, which was perfect for farming because the natives had followed the custom of burning the fields in the late fall to attract wild game, which they would then hunt. In 1651, "Dedham Village" became Medfield.

Natick

The Puritan missionary Rev. John Eliot, whom we met earlier, was responsible for the early settlement at Natick. He had begun his conversion of Native Americans in Newton, but the Massachusetts Bay Colony ceded land from Dedham in the southern part of what is now Natick, and the first Praying Town was set up there. In all, thirteen such towns were planned, but Natick became the political and spiritual center. It had a school, a form of government, and a meetinghouse, which was used by Eliot on his regular visits.

This all took place in the part of town now called South Natick. The Native Americans settled on both sides of the Charles and built a wooden bridge on a stone foundation between the banks and a village made up of three streets—today's Eliot, Union, and Pleasant. The meetinghouse stood where today's Eliot Church stands. The area is now part of the Broadmoor Wildlife Sanctuary.

Eliot's success in teaching and preaching lasted for more than two decades. But with the coming of King Philip's War in 1675, things changed. "King Philip" was really Metacomet, son of Massasoit, who became chief when his father died and attacked the settlers. As we have seen, the Praying Indians were restricted to Deer Island during the war, and when they returned to Natick they found that most of their possessions were gone, and the village never recovered. The land was sold off in pieces and most Native Americans drifted away.

Also along the Natick part of the Charles is a surprising wooden statue of a woman standing on a rock and praying. Carved by a sculptor named Daniel Sargent, people have told many stories about its origins, but according to author Mike Tougias, Sargent carved it to represent the Virgin Mary. The John Eliot Historical District in South Natick includes the homestead of Harriet Beecher Stowe, author of *Old Town Folks*, about South Natick as well as the better known *Uncle Tom's Cabin*.

Those who lived in the northern part of Natick wanted a church in the center, rather than supporting the Native American church to the south—this struggle was called the "Meetinghouse Dispute."

Pleasant Street Bridge, South Natick

Natick Center, Clark Building

Native Americans attacking a garrison house

Before the church could be moved to the center of town, Natick had to become a town, which it did in 1781.

When it was agreed to build a new meetinghouse in the center, those in the southern part of town did not want to support it. (This kind of dispute is common in the histories of various towns in the area.) They asked to be separated from the town, and in 1797 the General Court restored some land to Natick, but the south and east sections stayed part of Needham. The Native American church was abandoned, but in 1828 the Eliot Church was built on the site, the fifth church in that locale.

During the Revolution, Natick sent one out of three in its population to fight. Among the many who fought at Lexington and Bunker Hill, were a number of Praying Indians.

The Boston & Albany Railroad came through town in 1836 and this led to rapid growth in the shoe business. Just before the Civil War, the invention of the sewing machine brought a number of shoe factories to town. The industry hit its peak in 1880 with 23 factories producing the third-largest number of shoes in the country. These were mostly work shoes. In fact, Natick was famous for making a brogan used by soldiers during the Civil War.

Natick had another unique industry—H. Harwood and Sons made baseballs. The so-called "lively" ball that replaced the ones used in the "deadball era" originated in Natick in 1858. It used a wound core and was developed by John W. Walcott. The cover of the ball was held tightly in place with Harwood's figure eight stitching, devised by Col. William Cutler. It became the icon for the sport of baseball.

The baseballs made in the factory were made by hand by workers seated on a bench made for that purpose. Today, all baseballs for Major League Baseball are made in Costa Rica, but they are made in the same way, by hand, on similar benches. Machines could not provide the same quality.

In another burst of creativity, the world's first baseball factory, having fulfilled its usefulness, was converted to a BFC—a baseball factory condominium—in the center of Natick, overlooking the railroad station. The condo maintains its architectural integrity.

Three stagecoach routes stretched east-west through Natick on the Boston to Hartford route, each with its own village and tavern. The Felchville Tavern sat on the north road, Morse in the center, Eliakim Morrill Tavern in the south. The Peletiah Morse tavern still stands on Eliot Street. It boasts a red coat that was supposedly taken from a British soldier during the Lexington-Concord fracas.

Natick had two serious fires, near the time of the Great Fires of Chicago and Boston, the first in South Natick. The second, in Natick Center, had property damage greater in proportion of its value to the town than the Chicago Fire three years earlier. However, no lives were lost and the town quickly rebuilt.

Some, but certainly not all the people in Natick, supported what could be called iconic causes. It had many abolitionists, supporters of women's rights, and social reformers. A tunnel between the Walcott Mansion and the railroad tracks was used for the Underground Railroad. When John Brown led his raid on the armory at Harper's Ferry, a "Natick Resolution" was signed by many leaders protesting his execution.

Since its inception in 1897, the Boston Marathon, which begins in Hopkinton, runs for five miles through Natick along Route 135 while thousands watch.

As in other Greater Boston towns, the population grew by multiples after World War II, and had another boost when the Massachusetts Turnpike was built through the northern part of town. Commercial development has been greatest along Route 9. At the edge of Lake Cochichuate, Carling Brewery constructed a large building in 1957. It is now corporate headquarters of Boston Scientific.

Dover

Southeast of Natick, this small town was incorporated 200 years after its earliest settlement. Located on the south bank of the Charles, it has many springs and was first called Springfield Parish in 1748, when it was still part of Dedham. It became the Town of Dover in 1836. Dover still has its original meetinghouse, raised in 1754, and the home of its first minister, Benjamin Caryl, is on the register of National Historic Places.

Caryl served for half a century in this post.

The Sons of Liberty met in the tavern that belonged to Daniel Whiting, a veteran of the French and Indian Wars, who also shouldered a musket at the Lexington alarm.

Across the street was the Training Ground where the Minutemen of the town drilled before 66 of them marched off to the Battle Road on April 19, 1775.

One of them, Elias Haven, had been plowing his field and left his plow in place as he went off to battle where he was killed in the town of Menotomy (Arlington). Daniel Whiting, on the other hand, went on to fight at Bunker Hill where, as a major, he led a company and became a Lieutenant Colonel by war's end.

Another soldier to gain a degree of fame in the Revolution was Private Larabee, who is said to have helped to row George Washington across the ice-filled Delaware prior to his taking of Trenton. The Sawin Museum has his powder horn.

Though the Charles River at Dover had little potential energy, townsmen dammed it sufficiently to use it for mills that made nails and rolled iron early in the 1800s. Like nearby towns, Dover had craft industries in bonnets and boots.

Westwood

Lying east of Dover and south of Dedham, Westwood had its first settlers in 1640, when it was known as West Dedham. It was the last town to separate from Dedham, becoming incorporated in 1897. The intended name was "Nahatan," but the town of Nahant objected since the names were close. To expedite matters, the name was changed to Westwood.

It was a farming community until World War II, then became residential. In fact, Westwood was ranked 13th on the list of Best Places to Live in the United States by *Money* magazine in 2005.

Westwood is home to the Hale Reservation off Route 109, which has many miles of wilderness hiking trails.

The Charles River Basin

The term "Charles River Basin" refers here to the widest part of the river. It flows between Watertown and the mouth of the river at Boston Harbor. Even though it's wide, its gradient is so gradual that the current seldom flows with great speed. This allows it to serve as an urban water playground for Greater Bostonians.

From the New Dam at the Charlestown Bridge, west to the dam at Watertown Square, the Basin was conceived by Charles Eliot in the last decade of the nineteenth century as a public parkland. Today it has more than twenty parks and natural areas, and is edging closer to what Eliot probably had in mind.

Eliot, of course, was a seer and one of Frederick Law Olmsted's disciples. And he had a lot of work to do. His vision had to be formed as he looked at an area ridged with mud flats. It had a noxious odor, too.

But Eliot could see his way out of this morass. The keystone of his plan was the 1910 dam at the current Museum of Science. Once that was built it would be possible to keep the water at a fairly steady level, all the way out to Watertown.

The vision-building began with the dam. That was the firm basis for this mighty task, but it had lesser currents, too, as well as nice little frills and curlicues that would raise the Basin above the ordinary. The improvements ahead would bring pastoral scenery, recreational possibilities, and even an inner-city sanctuary.

Today the Basin is far different from the one John Winthrop cast a Puritanical gaze upon. Much of it is man-made, other aspects are not. The Charles now has flood control, which it lacked, but it still has plant and animal life that fit the ecology of this urban park. The width of the basin at Back Bay can readily be seen from the Cambridge side of the river, from which photographs are often taken.

Boston University dominates much of the Allston side of the Charles.

The development of the Basin began with the control of flooding and freshening of the waters from pollution that followed the filling in of the Back Bay in the late 1800s. The damming of the mouth of the river kept it fresh until the mid-twentieth century. Recent improvements have brought people back to the river for recreation and improved water quality as well.

It's not just the Bruins and Celtics that play defense at TD Garden. Behind the arena stands the dam for the Charles River that holds back the tidal inflow of salt water and controls the flow of the water level in the Charles River Basin.

The Citgo sign at Kenmore Square, a Boston icon, peers over the Green Monster at Red Sox games.

The Citgo sign is clearly seen from the Charles and beyond.

The Back Bay skyline features the Prudential Center and 111 Huntington with its open dome standing their watch on the Charles.

The early morning skyline reveals two Hancock Buildings standing as silent sentinels as a summer Sunday dawns.

The new dam replaces Eliot's earlier one at the Museum of Science, which held back the ocean tides until 1978, by which time the Eliot era was over.

The dam that Eliot deemed necessary brought Boston a (mostly) freshwater river basin and riverfront park called the Charles River Esplanade. The new dam also provides flood control—a need on the Charles since the 1960s. Six pumps keep the salt-water tides from invading the freshwater tidal basin and it has locks that allow small boats and larger ones to move from river to harbor just as a fish ladder does for the gilled population.

Clearly, the Charles River Basin we know today with its boating and bombastic fireworks and sculls from schools, is one that has been altered from the Olmsted and Eliot creations. So let's visit the evolution.

Frederick Law Olmsted, creator of Boston's "emerald necklace" believed that urban parks and green spaces ought to provide city dwellers with a place where they could renew their spirits. The present Charles River Basin fills this requirement and lives it large.

Olmsted's role in building the Basin began with his design for "Charlesbank" as he called the lawn on the Beacon Hill-Back Bay side of the river. An outdoor gymnasium that stood in front of Massachusetts General Hospital was part of it. The Esplanade was called the Boston Embankment, a grassland to which trees were later added along with recreation areas and facilities. It ran as far as the Harvard Bridge at Massachusetts Avenue.

The new Charles River Dam, with TD Garden and the Zakim-Bunker Hill Bridge, anchors the successful Charles River Basin.

The embankment was made wider and longer in the late 1920s and 1930s using a million-dollar gift by Helen Osborne Storrow in the name of her husband James, for whom the area was also named. The bigger area included the lagoon, beaches, boat landings, and a concert area, which was used for the first time in 1929 by Arthur Fiedler and the Boston Pops Orchestra.

More improvements were just ahead. The most memorable addition was the Hatch Memorial Shell, built in 1941 and used as a stage for the Pops in their summer concerts. The Hatch Shell has become so familiar to viewers of the televised July 4th concerts and fireworks displays that it has become an icon for Boston.

Another feature of the lower Charles is sailing, which began in the 1930s. The Esplanade boathouse was built in 1941 and Community Boating—the first program of its type in the country—began in 1946. Thousands have learned to sail there, and many others have learned to enjoy rowing at the Community Rowing site at the riverside Daly Rink in Brighton.

Not every improvement went smoothly. In fact, the attempt to build a road called Storrow Drive across the Esplanade ran into major opposition from residents and preservationists. The road would run along the river all the way out to Brighton. In the end, mitigation prevailed when additional islands and pathways were built to make up for the loss of parkland to the road.

In Brighton, between the Eliot Bridge and the Arsenal Street Bridge, Christian A. Herter Park was built. It has playgrounds, a public theater and boating. In the 1960s it was connected to the rest of the basin via the Dr. Paul Dudley White Bike Path that accommodate bikers, walkers, and runners. It forms an 18-mile loop along both sides of the river.

Skateboarders will be accommodated downstream at a skateboard park in Cambridge near the Zakim Bunker Hill Bridge being built by the Charles River Conservancy in conjunction with the state's Department of Conservation and Recreation (which is the successor of Eliot's Metropolitan District Commission. The skateboard park is part of a plan (by the MDC in 1997) for what is called the "New Basin"—the shoreline between the old dam and the new. Its restoration and amenities come and will come from mitigation funds for the Central Artery project over the Charles.

An 8.5-acre recreation spot known as North Point Park is part of this area—known as the "lost half mile" of the Charles.

The Hatch Shell, seen on television each July 4th, nestles between the river and downtown.

132

Yards of sail may usually be seen on both sides
of West Boston Bridge.

The new, and little-known, North Point Park is a tranquil Charlesbank gem seaward from the Museum of
Science at riverfront which serves as a front row for fireworks on the Fourth of July.

North Point Park is worth finding.

Bostonians who see the name of Eliot Bridge, or even those who simply enjoy the ambience of a relaxing day along the river, might pause in their reflection and renewal to give a quiet "Hosanna!" to Charles Eliot, whose vision made it all possible.

"Who's he?" they may ask. They could easily learn that he was one of many benefactors of theirs who has helped to make their lives more pleasurable. That may not have been his ultimate objective, but he certainly set out to make things better as benefactors have done since history has been recorded—perhaps even longer.

Maintenance, however, is an ongoing process in most things, and certainly in the river basin. Improved navigation, flood control, and recreation led to more development and increasing pollution. For example, Magazine Beach, which had long been a public beach in Cambridge upstream from the Boston University/Cottage Farm Bridge, often had to be closed because of pollution and was replaced by an MDC swimming pool.

Today the Charles River Basin parklands are owned and managed by the Department of Conservation and Recreation (DCR). Well over a million people make use of the recreational opportunities they offer each year. Besides the Independence Day concerts at the Hatch Shell, the basin hosts an annual Head of the Charles Regatta each fall, and other events.

In the year 2000, a citizen's advocacy group called the Charles River Conservancy was founded. It is dedicated to restoring and maintaining the Basin in cooperation with other groups. The group and its 2,000 volunteers have been working in that interval to enhance the ecology of the parklands and to make them more accessible. They consider Charles Eliot to be their guiding light.

North Point Park has a sunken stream, a tot lot,
and a wide lawn near the river.

The people who live along the Charles, and those from farther away as well, make plentiful use of the river for activities of all kinds. Once a mainstay for transportation and industry, the Charles River now acts as a magnet for those who wish to sail and scull, fish and frolic, listen to music and watch fireworks. It even serves as a playground for children. The river also serves those who like the possibility of moving through the heart of a great city on a ribbon of serenity among verdant parklands.

The Charles River Basin, with its beauty and all its activity, is perhaps the best-known area of the watershed. But, as we have seen, the entire river has its stories and its uses, serving for centuries as a kind of "Main Street" of Greater Boston. The Charles is the river that runs through it.

Paul Revere Park lies east of the Bunker Hill-Zakim Bridge, near the dam, and not far from the fireworks on the Fourth.

Paul Revere Park playground

Zakim-Bunker Hill Bridge marks the beginning of the harbor; TD Garden in the background bears the logo of the 2011 Stanley Cup Champions.

Clarke, George Kuhn, *History of Needham, Massachusetts 1711-1911*. (Cambridge, MA, Universty Press, 1912).

Crawford, Michael J., Natick: *A History of Natick 1650-1975*. (Natick, MA, Natick Historical Commission, 1979).

Haglund, Karl, *Inventing the Charles River*. (Cambridge, MA: MIT Press, 2003).

Hall, Max, *The Charles: The People's River*. (Boston: David Godine, 1986).

Higginson, Thomas Wentworth, *Old Cambridge*. (New York, MacMillan, 1899).

Jaffe, Eric, "The King's Best Highway," (Scribner, 2010).

King's Handbook of Newton. Copyright, 1889, by Moses King Corporation.

Kutlert, Stanley I., *Privilege and Creative Destruction: The Charles River Bridge Case*. (Baltimore: John Hopkins U. Press, 1971).

McAdow, Ron, *The Charles River*. (Marlborough, MA: Bliss Press, 1992).

Tougias, Michael, *Exploring the Hidden Charles*. (Boston, Appalachian Mountain Club Books, 1997).

Touglias, Michael, *The Hidden Charles*. (Emmaus, PA, Rodale Press, 1991).

Tourtelot, Arthur B., *The Charles*. (New York: Farrar & Rinehart, 1941).

Electronic Sources

Glaskin, Max, "Steam-powered car breaks century-old speed record," 2009-08-25, retrieved 2009-08-26, (www.wired.com/autopia/2009/08/british-steam-car-record-2).

"Newton Conservators: Long Walks and Bike Tours, The Charles River in North Newton," accessed May 6, 2011 (www.newtonconservators.org/longwalkscharlesnorth.htm).

Nonatum, Wikipedia. (http://en.wikipedia.org/wiki/Nonantum, Massachusetts).

"Nonantum: The Gateway to Newton," Adams Street Shul, Agudas Achim Anshei Sfard, accessed May 6, 2011 (www.adamsstreet.org/about-us/contact-us.html).

Miller, A. Richard, "1651–2001: 350th Anniversary of Natick, Massachusetts and the Natick Praying Indians," accessed May 5, 2011 (www.millermicro.com/natprayind.html).

Sobel, Erik, "The World's Fastest Canoe," accessed April 21, 2011 (www.steamcar.net/stanley/fastest.pdf).

Southwick, Arthur, "Waban the Wind" (http://wabanimprovement.org/oldsite/waban%20%%20days/wabanwind).

Index